LOVE IS ACTION
ESSAYS FROM AN AWARD-WINNING ALZHEIMER'S BLOG

earlyonset.blogspot.com

By

L. S. Fisher

MOZARK

www.MozarkPress.com

Published by Mozark Press, www.Mozarkpress.com
PO Box 1746, Sedalia, MO 65302

Cover Photo: 2019 Walk to End Alzheimer's, photo credit The Scarlett Lens Photography

Acknowledgement: Cover design and book layout by H.D. Ream

DISCLAIMER: *Statements or opinions expressed in the stories and articles of this publication are those of the author and do not necessarily represent the views or positions of any person or entity associated with publication of the book or the Alzheimer's Association.*

ISBN: 978-0-9903270-8-0

DEDICATION

Early Onset Alzheimer's Blog is dedicated to Jimmy D. Fisher and to all whose lives have been disrupted by a debilitating disease and to their families.

OTHER TITLES BY L. S. FISHER

Alzheimer's Anthology of Unconditional Love

Early Onset Blog
Essays from an Online Journal
(Ozark Writers League 2010 Book of the Year)

Early Onset Blog
The Friendship Connection and Other Essays

Early Onset Alzheimer's
Encourage, Inspire, and Inform

Early Onset Alzheimer's
My Recollections, Our Memories

Focus on the Positive

Garden of Hope

The Broken Road

At the End of the Day

The Heart Remembers

Treasure Trove of Memories

Ruminations of a Caregiver

Available at www.lsfisher.com

Table of Contents

Introduction

AT MY GRANDDAUGHTER'S wedding, the minister said that love is action, not an emotion. Love as action is the best way to describe the love of a caregiver for a spouse or other family member who has dementia.

Caregivers invest a lot of action into caring for a loved one with dementia. Through each stage of the disease, caregiving becomes more intense and time consuming. In the early stages, a care partner provides assistance and encouragement. As the disease progresses, the caregiver gradually takes on responsibility for providing more basic care.

In the late stages of Jim's life, he was a resident of a long-term care facility, but our family sprang into action. We pulled together to feed him and see to his comfort. I bathed him and provided his more personal care.

Alzheimer's can make a person feel helpless, but we embraced the opportunity to make a difference and walked annually in the Walk to End Alzheimer's. Taking action was an extension our love. Jim's Team has walked in every walk since 1998. For the first few years, Jim walked with us. I still feel his presence at every walk.

Advocacy is another action that shows a caregiver's love. It requires dedication and patience to be an Alzheimer's advocate. The Alzheimer's Impact Movement has streamlined the advocacy process and has increased the efficiency and success of our legislative contacts. Hundreds of determined advocates wearing purple sashes, armed with facts and figures, create a stir on Capitol Hill. We share our personal stories and listen to our legislator's personal stories. We seldom meet anyone who hasn't known the heartbreak of Alzheimer's. Almost everyone we meet has a parent, a spouse, a grandparent, sibling, aunt, uncle, or beloved friend who has dementia.

We need to take action to end this disease. The action we take may be physical—Walking to End Alzheimer's, wearing a purple sash and going to our state or nation's capital, writing a letter to the editor, posting on Facebook, or picking up the phone to call about an upcoming bill. The action may be as simple as writing a check.

At the heart of the actions we take is our love for those living with dementia and the loved ones we've lost to dementia. Our actions pave the way to a world without Alzheimer's disease.

~ Linda Fisher

TREASURE HUNT

ALTHOUGH I'M A DECLUTTER class dropout, I've been tackling the piles of storage tubs in my basement. A person my age has a long time to accumulate a wide variety of items. I've filled a half dumpster of old paperwork, things I just don't want anymore, worn outdated clothing, and worthless souvenirs.

The process is slow, but I don't want to resort to the strategy a friend of mine used when she sorted through her deceased husband's storage boxes. She spent weeks going through his things, but finally decided to dump the rest without looking inside the boxes. I don't fault her for this at all. The hardest part of decluttering is knowing what to throw away, knowing what to keep, and how to dispose of the rest.

In the midst of wondering why I hadn't thrown mountains of stuff away years ago, I've found unexpected treasures. I found a lost photo of Jim holding his M-16 in Vietnam. I found a box of ribbons for our Alzheimer's Walk Committee's participation in parades. I found a box of magazine and newspaper articles I'd saved but hadn't put in the scrapbooks from the five years that I coordinated the "Memory Walk."

Recently, we found a scrapbook my husband's mom had made with photos of family members with neatly handwritten captions. I considered it a real treasure. His cousins dropped by for a visit, and I showed the scrapbook to them. My husband, an only child without children of his own said, "Nobody is going to want this when I'm gone."

Therein lies the dilemma. Our generation's treasure is trash for the generation following us. Although my sons value some mementos, they have no room in their homes for all my stuff, especially things that mean nothing to them. Along with the items in the basement, I have several collections. Some have at least garage-sale value and others, well, not so much.

I floated the idea that my sons should hold my memorial services at Christmastime and give everyone attending a nutcracker. "Give the big ones to people that I don't like," I said.

My daughter-in-law quipped, "Gives an entirely new meaning to 'parting gift.' "

The best thing to come out of my treasure hunt was finding one of Jim's guitars that had been in a "hidey-hole" for the past eighteen years. I gave it to my brother to use for as long as he wants. We practiced the songs for our monthly nursing home gig and for my mom's birthday party. It really warmed my heart to see someone playing Jim's guitar. When my brother sang "Sing Me Back Home," I told him that the guitar could probably play that tune by itself. "Maybe that's why it sounded so good this time," he said.

Going through the clutter, has been a time of remembrance of good times and hard times. Of course, now I must press on to get past that stage of mass chaos. One of my motivations is the thought that someday someone may just dump the storage tubs into a dumpster without looking at the contents.

LIFE WAS SIMPLE

1956

I TOOK MY DOG out yesterday in forty mile an hour winds. Well, sometimes I took her out and other times, I huddled behind the glass storm door. I opened the door a crack to tug on her leash, and the wailing wind reminded me of nights at my grandma's house when I was a little girl. As I huddled in a feather bed beneath quilts that weighed more than I did, I could hear the whistle of the north wind as it whipped around the house and through the ill-fitted windows.

This morning during breakfast, my husband and I talked about poverty. I said, "I never worry about being poor, because I've been there and it doesn't scare me."

"You know, we don't really need most of the stuff in this house. We could live without cell phones, Dish Network, fancy TV's, iPads, Kindles...," he said.

After our discussion, I began to think about how life was so much simpler when I was growing up. Playtime didn't involve deciding which toy to choose, because I didn't have many. Instead, I would decide which tree to climb. It wasn't hard to choose what to wear. I had two choices—one of my three or four school dresses, or the old clothes I wore at home. When I was little, I had two pair of shoes (school and play), and in the summertime, I went barefoot most of the time.

No one had heard of Alzheimer's. When my elderly great-aunt developed dementia, folks just said she was "slipping." We kids enjoyed her childlike behavior and loved her unconditionally.

After Jim and I married, we had a black-and-white 19-inch TV. We struggled to pay the bills, lived in rental houses, and bought clothes at garage sales, or I made them. For several years, we didn't even have a phone because it was an extra expense. We had one old car after we sold the other to pay my hospital bill when my son was born.

We never obsessed about being poor. Just like my folks, we never resorted to food stamps, government assistance, or borrowing money to help us through the lean times. Instead, we saved all we could, so we could make it on our own.

Life was simpler and people were kinder. We didn't have politics shoved down our throats twenty-four hours a day. We voted and then let it go until the next election. We didn't have our friends and family insulting our intelligence on Facebook every day because we made different political choices. If someone mentioned a tweet, we'd have been looking for a bird.

Our social activity was visiting with family and listening to their foot-stomping country music. We went to a laid-back country church on Sunday. Family relationships were cherished, and we would never deliberately be unkind or critical of them.

Jim's mom always said, "If I have food on the table and a roof over my head, I'm content." Simple goals, important goals, considering she had temporarily lived under a tree, more than once, and under a bridge at another point in time. She never felt homeless and as long as she was surrounded by family, their love shored her up and made her fearless about poverty.

No, poverty doesn't scare me. Sitting around the old oak table drinking home-squeezed lemonade seems much more appealing that working my butt off trying to keep up with all my obligations.

This morning, when I took the dog out for her morning walk, I told her, "Yesterday's wind is gone, just like the simple times." She stopped, tilted her head, and had that look on her face that indicated she thought I was maybe, just maybe, talking about the treat in my pocket.

BRIGHT SHINY OBJECT

AFTER NINE DAYS OF bitter, cold weather and gloomy skies, I walked the dog outside and wondered…*what is that bright shiny object casting shadows upon the earth?* I welcomed the rays of sunshine and the tiny amount of warmth it psychologically added to the day.

I immediately thought of how lately I'd heard the idiom "bright shiny object" to describe people who have risen quickly in the world of politics. In other words, they are saying these young, energetic politicians are charismatic but not long lasting or particularly useful.

Sometimes older workers can have this same attitude toward new employees. When I found a job at the electric cooperative, I was the youngest person in the office. My job was to learn how to operate that new fangled computer. A minority of the employees were suspicious of me because they thought I was hired so they could be replaced with a machine. I was a bright and shiny object in their world, and they would have liked nothing better than to sandblast the shine. Fortunately, most employees thought I was useful and non-threatening, and they polished the shine.

I came to know and love my co-workers as family, and they inspired me to be a polisher rather than a sandblaster. I am happy for my friends and family when they succeed. Life is tough enough without sandblasters purposely trying to take someone down.

To refer to someone as a bright shiny object should never have been a derogatory term. The definition of bright means "full of light." I believe that Alzheimer's caregivers are full of light. They've had their lives sandblasted by a devastating disease, but accepted the responsibility and challenge of caring for loved ones. Research shows that Alzheimer's caregivers provide more hours of care and a higher level of assistance with activities of daily living than caregivers for persons without dementia. One in three Alzheimer's caregivers reported that their own health deteriorated. Yet, each year, more than 16 million family and friend caregivers provide more than 18 billion hours of care for their loved ones with dementia.

Shiny has two definitions that I thought noteworthy—(1) worn or rubbed smooth, (2) reflecting light. Alzheimer's advocates are often caregivers or former caregivers. Advocates can be worn slick from years of caregiving, but they get the importance of advocacy. Some are a voice for their loved ones with dementia, but others are the voices of persons living with dementia. Becoming an advocate is a positive reaction to a negative situation. The Alzheimer's Impact Movement (AIM), the advocacy arm of the Alzheimer's Association, has driven policymakers to address the crisis of Alzheimer's disease. AIM advocates have diligently worked for years to bring national awareness of Alzheimer's disease and increased research funding.

An object is a goal. The ultimate goal is to find a cure for Alzheimer's, so that future generations will eventually forget the wreckage Alzheimer's leaves in its wake. The Alzheimer's Association is the largest worldwide non-profit funder of Alzheimer's research. The NIH (National Institutes of Health) has steadily increased their Alzheimer's funding. A worldwide effort to end Alzheimer's disease adds to the hope that a cure will be discovered sooner, rather than later.

These bright shiny objects have staying power and are extremely necessary in the fight against Alzheimer's. Caregivers overcome adversity to be full of unconditional love and light, advocates reflect the light and take AIM at engaging policymakers to make Alzheimer's a priority, and researchers seek a clear and obtainable goal to end Alzheimer's.

The clouds roll in again, and I wonder *where is that bright and shiny object that brings light and life to the world?* The clouds may hide it from view, but it steadfastly shines, patiently waiting to burn through the gloom to brighten the world with hope.

SILVER ALERT

I HAD SO MANY events on my calendar this week that I was on the verge of overload meltdown. I had appointments, two meetings that I needed to prepare for, a luncheon I couldn't attend because of a conflict with the other two meetings, a conference call, and music practice.

The weather was fine on Monday, one appointment finished, check. On Tuesday, due to a predicted ice storm, one of the Thursday meetings was cancelled, check.

Wednesday, the ice came. Every tree, shrub, and blade of grass turned to silver. I couldn't step out of the door because of solid ice. I had taken a hard fall on the ice several years ago, so safety first! My dog had to stay within the bounds of her 25-foot leash. She slid on the concrete drive and gingerly stepped on the grass. Each blade was an ice-covered prong that affected her balance and distracted her from her daily routine.

Wednesday night, the weather alert radio went off. In addition to our ice alert, severe thunderstorm warnings were issued. Before long, we had high winds, pouring down rain, thunder and lightning. This is Missouri after all. Another meeting cancelled for Thursday, check. Conference call and luncheon cancelled, check, check. Practice cancelled for Friday, check.

Thursday morning, the power went out for a few hours. After daylight, I noticed the tree in the front yard was mostly laying on the ground. The sun came out for a few minutes and the ice, though treacherous, turned our yard into a silver wonderland. Since my responsibilities had been cancelled for the day, I read, played my computer game, and took a nap. Time for myself, check.

Although in the past, I often ignored weather alerts, it seems that our meteorologists are more accurate now.

In this case, the prediction of ice, our silver alert, was spot on.

Weather isn't the only thing that can be predicted with accuracy. Silver alerts for missing, vulnerable adults will be needed throughout the United States. Six out of ten people with dementia wander, and Jim was one of those who seemed to be seeking something that was in a different place than where he was at the time.

Indicators that predict wandering: a person who paces, exhibits repetitious behavior, forgets how to find familiar places, is gone longer than necessary when going for a walk or driving, gets anxious when in crowded stores or malls, or keeps looking for an undefined object.

I know that when Jim wandered off, there was a fine line between checking where he usually went and panicking because I couldn't easily find him. Everyone in our neighborhood knew to call me if they saw Jim walking alone. We installed alarms on the door, enrolled him in Safe Return, and tried to be vigilant at all times, but he still managed to wander off. He wandered off in an airport, Silver Dollar City, a mall, from a cabin on vacation, and other places too numerous to mention.

You should look no more than fifteen minutes before you enlist professional help. I notified security at the mall and at Silver Dollar City. If no official security is available, call 911 and file a vulnerable adult missing persons report. The authorities will help you find your loved one and can issue a silver alert. If your loved one is enrolled in the Medic Alert + Alzheimer's

Association Safe Return®, you should notify them at 800-625-3780.

When you are aware of a Silver Alert, share the information on social media. The more people who are looking, the more likely the missing person will be found safely. Silver Alerts have a high success rate!

If you are a caregiver, it is easy to be overwhelmed with the responsibility of looking after the safety of your loved one. Squeeze in some precious time for yourself. It is amazing how one day, one hour, or even thirty minutes can re-energize your body and spirit.

BROKEN SURVIVORS

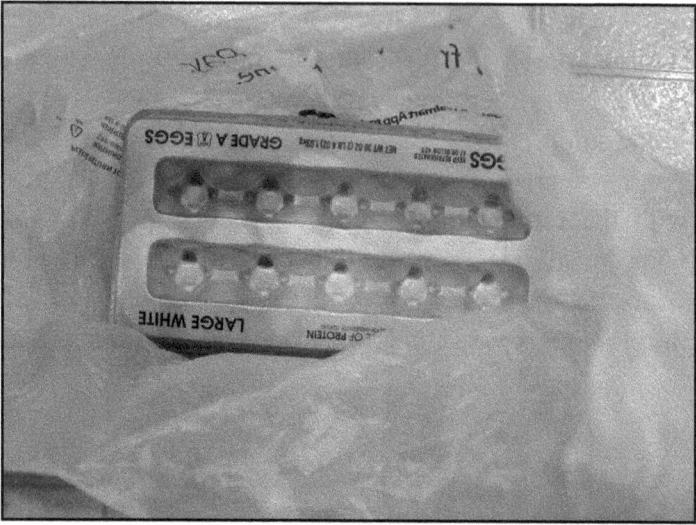

AS I BROUGHT IN groceries from my car, I looked like a bag lady. I carried as many bags as I could to cut down on the number of trips from the garage to the kitchen. Yesterday, I juggled four bags into the house. I manhandled the gallon of milk and a sack of cans onto the counter. I lifted the lighter bag with a carton of eggs in it and prepared to set it beside the other bags. The plastic bag slipped out of my hands and the eggs fell to the floor.

I heard a distinct splat and knew that some of the eggs had prematurely met a sad end. I picked up the carton and at first glance, they all looked fine. One by one, I plucked the eggs out of the carton and examined them. Of the eighteen eggs, fourteen were broken on the bottom, but four had survived unscathed.

The eggs all suffered the same disaster and all the eggs were fragile. It seems to me that the fate of the eggs is a life lesson. Not one single person makes it through life without catastrophe.

Your struggles are different from mine. Your heartaches, failures, insecurities, relationships, health problems, and worries are different. Everything that happened in your life—good and bad—made you the unique person you are. How well you overcome adversity determines whether you are a survivor or a victim.

I've noticed that ninety-nine things could go right, but the one thing that goes wrong will haunt me. I can remember how hyped I was when the Alzheimer's Association chapter office decided to give *Alzheimer's Anthology of Unconditional Love* to our state legislators. I had collected stories from caregivers and persons with dementia, and the chapter staff chose the best stories to include in the book. I spent about a year on the project and invested my energy into editing the heart-felt stories.

I was recognized on the floor of the Missouri house and received a House Resolution from my representative. What should have been one of the happiest days in my life was ruined when a fellow advocate met me in the hallway. "If my chapter hadn't told me to give away this book, I wouldn't have because…" She went on to say something that wasn't true. I tried to show her where she was mistaken, but she wasn't interested in what I had to say. She had already made up her mind and didn't even hear me. That one negative comment stung, and I came close to deciding in that moment that I wasn't going to publish any more books.

It's obvious that this one negative Nelly did not change the trajectory of my life. I overcame my self-doubt and began blogging shortly after this experience. The day I started my blog, I thought long and hard before pushing that "publish" button.

One of the biggest hurdles to overcome if you want to leave the past behind is self-doubt. We all fail and fall short of our aspirations. If you notice someone who apparently leads a charmed life, just know that appearances can be deceptive. Survivors are often broken people who pick up the pieces and glue them back together. Human survivors may look fine on the outside, but inside, they hurt from unhealed wounds.

I cracked one of those "survivor" eggs into the skillet this morning. The egg looked perfect on the outside, but the yolk was broken and it was scrambled on the inside.

Memory Day 2019

THE TYPICAL MISSOURI WEATHER forecast called for a possibility of ice on Memory Day. The night before, Jessica and I held a text discussion trying to decide how early we had to leave to make it to the Capitol on time. To complicate things, the Capitol Building was undergoing renovations and only one entrance was open.

My husband watched me busily texting, as I told him the various times under consideration. "Well, we decided to leave at 8:00," I said.

After I put the phone down, he asked, "Where are you meeting?"

"Well, since we didn't decide anything different, I assume we will meet at the same place we meet every year."

About that time, Jessica sent another message. "We didn't decide where we were meeting."

After all our weather worries, the ice stayed away, and we had an uneventful trip to the Capitol. Soon we met with other purple clad advocates. We made new friends and reunited with advocates we had met previously. Several hugs later, we split up into teams to visit our senators and representatives. Jessica, Mark, Samantha, and I donned our purple sashes, put on our figurative advocacy hats, and set off to keep our appointments.

We had two asks this year: Fund Alzheimer's Grants for Respite and Pass the Structured Family Caregiver Act. It was easy for me to support both bills wholeheartedly.

Every caregiver needs time away to refresh and rejuvenate. The state of Missouri has awarded $450,000 in Alzheimer's Grants for respite for several years in the past, and we asked for the same amount again. Of the Missourians receiving respite funds, 99% report they can keep their loved one at home longer. By delaying nursing home placement by a mere two months, the state could save $2 million in Medicaid costs. What a deal!

We also asked our legislators to pass the Structured Family Caregiver Act. This pilot program offers a new option under Medicaid for full-time caregivers. The caregiver would have the support of an in-home agency that would provide professional support. The family would receive care planning, training, remote monitoring, and monthly visits. The caregiver would receive a daily stipend to help relieve financial hardship. The goal of this program is to keep persons with Alzheimer's and related dementia at home rather than in nursing homes. The cost to the state would be about half the cost of a long-term care facility.

Alzheimer's is the most expensive disease in America for both the government and the families who care for loved ones with the disease. The cost of incontinent supplies alone would strain the budget of a Medicaid eligible household. Imagine the plight of a low-income family dealing with a high cost disease.

At the end of our visits, we attended the Memory Day Ceremony in the Rotunda. Governor Parson talked about his personal experience with Alzheimer's and pledged his support. Advocate Terri Walker spoke about receiving her diagnosis on her grandson's birthday. Her well-spoken words had the power to touch our hearts. Her youth, sparkling eyes, fabulous haircut, and lovely purple dress served well to strip away any preconceived stereotypes of the face of Alzheimer's.

Families dealing with Alzheimer's need our support, our hugs, and our advocacy. Until we find a cure for Alzheimer's, I will continue to join other committed advocates at the Missouri Capitol and on Capitol Hill in Washington, D.C.

AS TIME GOES BY

WELL, YESTERDAY WE MADE the big switch to Daylight
Saving Time. At my age, any change isn't easy, and I
sure miss that hour.

It seems as if time goes by quicker each day. I only
have my Christmas decorations as far as the landing,
waiting to go into their storage boxes. My snowmen are
still sitting on the ledge although, gee, it hasn't snowed
in a week. Our first almost-spring rain melted the last of
the snow in the yard as long ago as yesterday. Where
has the time gone? St. Patty's day is less than a week
away and Easter is on the horizon.

I believe that the busyness of life hides more hours than the one we lost between Saturday and Sunday. Juggling several projects at one time means I'm constantly putting out fires. Sometimes, I make progress and feel like I'm attacking the fires with a high-pressure fire department hose. More often than not, I look at the growing to-do list and might as well be beating back the flames with a gunnysack, and one that isn't even wet.

Where has the time gone? I look at the year 2019 and realize how vividly I can remember events of fifty years ago. This is the year of a golden anniversary that will never happen. Jim's life was cut short by an Alzheimer's type of dementia—a disease I had never heard of—corticobasal ganglionic degeneration.

CBGD is a rare disease that attacks the cerebral cortex and the basal ganglia in the brain. The onset usually occurs between the ages of 45 and 70 with an average duration of six or seven years. After he looked at Jim's autopsy report, his neurologist explained that CBGD is a movement disorder. Initial symptoms are usually difficulty walking because of stiffness, shakiness, or balance problems. This is usually followed with problems with speech and comprehension.

For some reason, Jim's earliest noticeable symptoms were with memory and speech. Early in the disease, he developed aphasia from the damage to his brain. He had trouble speaking and understanding words. Jim also had alien limb syndrome, especially in his right hand. He had to have his little finger amputated due to infection caused from clinching the hand he forgot how to use. He also had ideomotor apraxia (IMA) that resulted in his feet appearing to stick to the floor causing him to lose his balance.

I was relieved to learn that CBGD is almost always sporadic and not inherited. A variant in the tau gene is associated with a predisposition to CBGD, meaning it can occur more often in some families. However, not all people with CBGD have the tau gene variant, and not all people with the variant develop CBGD.

Jim passed away in 2005 after ten years of living with CBGD. Next month marks the fourteenth year anniversary of his death. Where did the years go? Sometimes, it seems a different lifetime, a different me. Other times, it takes my breath away as the realization that he is forever gone batters my heart anew. The pain is physical in those moments, and I can almost feel life slipping away.

How did seconds turn into minutes, and minutes into hours? How did twenty-four of those hours turn into days? How did the days turn into years? How many years will you and I have in a lifetime? The questions remain the same, but the answers are the biggest mystery of all.

RING OF FIRE

A FEW DAYS AGO, I was listening to some songs on my Kindle in an attempt to find something to sing with the Capps Family Band at our nursing home gigs. I listened to Patsy Cline, Emmylou Harris, Ray Price, Jim Reeves…and the list goes on. Eventually, I went out of YouTube and decided to go to bed.

After I was ready for bed, I woke up my Kindle and clicked on the Book tab. I heard the intro to the Johnny Cash version of "Ring of Fire" with its unmistakable mariachi horns. The music stopped when I opened the book I'd been reading. The book? *Ring of Fire* by Brad Taylor.

Some might call that a coincidence, but my goose bumps classified the experience as more "weird" than "coincidental." It seemed it was a message of some kind, but I didn't have a clue as to what it could possibly mean.

So if we think of love circled with a fiery ring, I believe you could say that nothing could penetrate that ring to destroy the all-consuming love within its circle. However you look at it, fire in the song is symbolic. Fire has many symbolic meanings, and I found the one that could mean something to me: Issues you are consumed by—a strong passion or prolonged obsession. Regardless of that stalker-esque phrase, I choose to relate it to my passion for being an Alzheimer's advocate.

I contacted the Alzheimer's Association soon after Jim was diagnosed with an Alzheimer's type of dementia. They connected me to a support group. Both the local chapter and the national Alzheimer's Association sent newsletters. Through the newsletters, I learned about a walk in our hometown known then as the "Memory Walk." Jim and I registered for the walk and on walk day discovered we were the only ones from our town. The next year, I became an Alzheimer's volunteer and coordinated our local walk.

When my daughter-in-law and I tried to get corporate sponsors, we realized that people didn't know much about Alzheimer's. They often referred to it as "old timers" disease. They thought age caused it and it just happened to elderly people. No big deal—just a part of growing old. The first priority was to educate them that Alzheimer's was a degenerative brain disease.

I went to Washington, DC, for the Alzheimer's Forum for the first time in 2001. By then, Jim had been in long-term care for a year. We advocates asked for $1 billion for Alzheimer's research and for legislation to help the families dealing with Alzheimer's. It didn't take long for me to find out that most senators and representatives didn't know much more about Alzheimer's disease than the folks back home. After much persuasive talk, we got a tiny fraction of our lofty goal. This pattern was repeated year after year. Sometimes we gained a small amount, other times we held steady, but a few times, our funding was decreased.

A lot of things have changed since my first trip to DC. As I look forward to my 19th trip next week, I know we will meet with legislators who know exactly what Alzheimer's is and how devastating it is to the families and to our government. Our senators and representatives are important partners in the fight to end Alzheimer's.

Yes, we've won many battles, but now we need to win the war. Current research funding for Alzheimer's is beyond our wildest dreams of nineteen years ago. The National Alzheimer's Plan was passed in 2012 to find an effective treatment or cure by 2025. It seemed like we had plenty of time to meet our goals, but time has gone by with promising treatments falling short of the target.

We must fund *successful* research and break through the ring of fire that separates Alzheimer's disease from a cure. In the meantime, we need to surround persons with dementia and care partners with a circle of love and caring.

Before Johnny Cash recorded "Ring of Fire," he had a dream of the mariachi horns. He made his dream come true by taking action. Well, I have dreams too, and I plan to take action at the Alzheimer's Advocacy Forum on April 2.

CHERRY BLOSSOMS AND SOARING KITES

MY TRIP TO THE ALZHEIMER'S Forum this year coincided with the Cherry Blossom Festival and the Blossom Kite Festival. It so happened that when my traveling buddy Jennifer and I ventured out, we ran into human traffic jams every step of the way. It was a little claustrophobic at times, especially when we were stuck at the metro exit behind a crowd of slow moving people.

Capitol Hill didn't seem quite as congested as usual this year, and for the most part, the security lines moved at a decent pace. It helped that we weren't rushed between our appointments.

After our forum training and updates on all things Alzheimer's, we were prepared to speak of Alzheimer's as the public health crisis it has become. We had four asks for our legislators:

1) Increase Alzheimer's research funding at the National Institutes of Health (NIH) by $350 million for fiscal year 2020. Currently, 5.8 million Americans are living with Alzheimer's disease. Without a medical breakthrough, that number will triple in a generation!

2) Support $20 million in fiscal year 2020 to implement the BOLD Infrastructure for Alzheimer's Act at the Centers for Disease Control and Prevention (CDC). BOLD will establish Alzheimer's and Related Dementias Public Health Centers of Excellence, fund public health departments, and increase data analysis and timely reporting.

3) Co-sponsor the Improving HOPE for Alzheimer's Act (S. 880/H.R. 1873). In 2017, only 1% of seniors living with Alzheimer's received the Medicare care planning benefit. We must educate providers and individuals with dementia about available care planning services.

4) Co-sponsor the Younger-Onset Alzheimer's Disease Act (S. 901/HR 1903). This would allow individuals with younger-onset dementia to receive services provided under the Older Americans Act, currently available only to Americans over the age of 60.

Our first visit of the day was with Senator Blunt who has become a champion for Alzheimer's. He greeted us, began to speak of the tremendous cost of Alzheimer's, and compared it to the defense budget.

Next, the Missouri delegation attended the Senate Hearing on Alzheimer's disease. In his remarks, Senator Hawley recognized our fellow advocate Lonni Schicker and briefly told about her younger-onset diagnosis. After the hearing, we visited his office.

My last meeting of the day was with Congresswoman Vicky Hartzler's office. I only met with her briefly since she had to go to the floor for a vote. We finished our visit with her senior legislative assistant, Bryan McVae.

After speaking to our legislators, we came away with the feeling that we are in this battle together. This is different from when we used to have to spend all our time convincing them that Alzheimer's affects all of us in one way or another. Our hopes are flying as high as a Blossom Festival kite that by working together, we can, and will, find a cure.

For the past few years, I've stayed an extra night to avoid the nail biting rush to the airport. I'd much rather be way early than just a few minutes too late to catch a flight home. At the airport, we came across some fellow advocates for a "selfie." Then, we disbursed to our separate homes to continue the fight to end Alzheimer's.

CRUEL APRIL

SOME DATES ARE SEARED into our memories and leave scars on our hearts. For me, that date is April 18, 2005.

When I flipped my calendar to April, I didn't think of flowers, thunderstorms, morel mushrooms, or even mowing the grass. I mentally, went back in time and remembered that April was the cruel month...when the beginning melded into the end. The good guy lost, and the relentless disease won.

I'd been so busy this month that it didn't seem possible that today was already the eighteenth day of the month. The month began in Washington DC at the Alzheimer's Forum. Then, there was the catching up to do with all the projects I'd put on hold to take time away, including the annual scourge known as taxes.

Today, the eighteenth of April, was a busy day. At nine o'clock this morning, I drove to Versailles for a

50-year class reunion committee meeting. Reconnecting with my former classmates has been a positive experience. As usual, when our work was done, we went to lunch.

After lunch, I picked up my mom and my aunt to go to the nursing home for our monthly music gig. We began setup at 2:00, and began our hour-long program at 2:30. One of my former classmates had brought some scanned photos for the reunion book and stayed to watch the program. "This is a lot of talent in one family," she said.

My mom and I had a short visit over a cup of coffee, and then I headed home. The sun was setting in the west by the time I pulled into the garage. The day was almost done. The black aura lifted some as the day dwindled down.

Tonight, I put the leash on the dog, slipped on my coat, and stepped out into the darkness. The clouds parted and the moon slid into view.

As often happens in the still of the night, I was left with my thoughts, my memories. The sorrow seeped into the fiber of my being, and hid beneath the surface. I thought of how Jim had always been a part of my life, and always would be. I remembered how Jim, a man of faith, told me that death was merely closing one door and opening another.

A cold breeze sent shivers through my body. It was as if he had whispered to my heart: the end has melded into the beginning, and the good guy won after all.

THE ROAD LESS TRAVELED

A GROUP OF MY FORMER classmates and I are planning our fifty year class reunion. Several have brought in photos taken on our senior trip to the Smoky Mountains. As they look at the tiny, blurry photos and reminisce, I realize how little I remember about the trip. I remembered the Grand Ole Opry. I remembered the towns of Gatlinburg and Chattanooga, Tennessee. I remembered traveling to the top of the mountain in a cable car. But as far as the shenanigans—the fake gun fight, the bathroom window on the bus falling out, a group going out looking for a place to bowl and getting stopped by the local police—I have zero recollection.

"I know I wasn't drunk, so I don't know why I can't remember all the things you remember," I said to the group.

"I can't remember much about it either," Cindy admitted.

Maybe the reason the memory of the senior trip faded so quickly for me was because Jim and I traveled so much. We always went west, but once in a while I would suggest the Smoky Mountains, but it just didn't work into our plans.

Now, oddly enough, on close to the fiftieth anniversary of the senior trip, we will be taking our girls' trip to South Carolina. On the way, we will be going through the Smoky Mountains. For me, this is an area I haven't been to in half a century. It seems just a little odd that I had reminisced with my former classmates, and then drove a few blocks to my mom's house to plan a trip to the same area.

One thing I'm sure of—a lot will have changed in fifty years. If nothing else, *I* have changed. I can't help but wonder if I'll visit certain sites that will bring about a feeling of déjà vu. Will the places call forth events stored in locked parts of my brain? Will I feel sadness for those in the class of '69 who now reside in eternity and not with us?

I have heard that some of my former classmates have memory problems. I don't know that anyone has been diagnosed with dementia, but then not everyone receives a diagnosis. According to the statistics, one in ten of us will develop Alzheimer's in our lifetimes. We have already reached the age of vulnerability, and are too old for younger onset dementia.

It's a little bit concerning that I can't remember much at all about the senior trip, but it would be devastating to not know the people I love. Recently,

I've visited with two men who held an important role in my life. One looked at me and said, "I don't know who you are." So, I told him who I was. The other gave me a hug, but never talked or showed any recognition in his eyes. You have to hate a disease that does that to people you love.

Although it made me sad, I didn't regret seeing either of them. One, I was told, was just having a bad day. The other, I was told, can't remember anything anymore. His family is just spending time with him and helping him enjoy life as much as they can.

Unfortunately, the road less traveled is often the one that leads to special care units in nursing homes. Excuses abound, but sometimes people just don't have the fortitude to give unconditional love to those who no longer seem to know who they are.

In the end, when they can't remember you, you still remember them. If the person you are hesitating to visit played a major role in your life, you are cheating yourself. If you don't share hugs, words of love, and bring a smile to someone's face, *you* are the big loser.

Travel that road. Take the time to hold fast to the memories that linger in your heart. Life has robbed a person with dementia of their memories, and he lives only in the moment. The more moments you share with your loved one, the more happiness you bring into his life, and yours. As we travel through life, we need to enjoy the journey before we reach the final destination.

LIFE IS...

I JUST WENT ON a nine-day vacation with my mom and sisters—our Girls Trip 2019. We had a relaxing time in both the mountains and on the beach. Nine days without thinking about obligations brings to mind that...

Life Is Good: In Savannah, GA, we took a trolley tour of old Savannah. Our one stop was at the Riverwalk. We ate lunch at the Shrimp Factory and visited a couple of shops. One of them, Fannie's Your Aunt, offered Life Is Good t-shirts. I found two that caught my eye and both had to do with music. Since I've joined the Capps Family Band, I practice my songs while I walk the dog. Did you know that singing lowers stress and helps with mental health? Singing also boosts memory.

Life Is Exasperating: Back home, life settled into the normal routine. Get up, take the dog out, fix breakfast, clean up, etc., etc. Most of all, I spent hours and hours trying to catch up on all the work I skipped out on while enjoying my vacation. Isn't that the downside of vacation? I've never had those little elves come in and do my work while I'm out of town.

Life Is Predictable: I can't help but notice that life is predictable. I can always count on the predictability of a normal day. The sun comes up every morning in the east and sets in the west. It rains from time-to-time, usually when we need to do outside work, and the grass grows faster than we can cut it. This was going to be the year we kept ahead of it—until it rained and rained and rained. We can't mow our lawn when the yard has the squishiness of a rice paddy.

Life Is Scary: It's hard to go through a very long period without a heart-stopping close call on the highway. There's nothing quite as fun as topping a hill and seeing cars headed your way in both lanes. Even in the safety of my home, I've had a few scares—one as recently as this morning. I was cooking breakfast and sipping my coffee while I watched the sausage brown. Normal early morning…until…I realized the kitchen was filling up with smoke. I turned around and smoke billowed from beneath the cabinets and along the countertop. I opened cabinet doors although I couldn't figure out how a fire could start in the cabinets.

"Harold, Harold!" I yelled. "There's smoke everywhere and I can't figure out where it's coming from!" He came into the kitchen, looked around, calmly, which by-the-way, was totally irritating when I was in a panic. He reached over and unplugged the toaster where our normally pale toast that has to be pushed down twice was completely charred.

Life Is Mysterious: I could regale you with stories of mysterious events in my life, but that would be a book of its own. Just this week, I was washing dishes and began to sing "Que Sera Sera," which to be honest, I hadn't even thought of in years. The next day, Doris Day passed away. Just a little odd, I thought. Last night, Harold was watching an old Law and Order rerun on the TV in the bedroom, and I decided to catch up on the pile of newspapers I hadn't read. I sat down on the couch in our kitchen and picked up a random newspaper. An article about the measles caught my eye. As I began to read, I could hear the medical examiner on the TV program "testifying" about how a child had died from the measles. As I read the next two lines, I was reading the words she was using to testify. That was mysterious and a little bit creepy.

Life Is Not Fair: I always try to be fair, but there isn't too much fair about life. Good people have terrible things happen to them and bad people have prosperity and lead charmed lives. That's just the way it goes. Jim was a good person and certainly did not deserve to have a horrible disease that robbed him of his most precious memories.

Life Is Attitude: How you look at life determines how life looks at you. If you see the negative, the negative consumes you. If you see the positive and spiritual uplifting side of life, it returns the favor. Life *is* good if you allow it to be.

ONE OF THESE THINGS

WHEN I FIRST STARTED elementary school, our workbook had pictures of objects, and the assignment was to choose the one that was different and did not belong. We would color the pictures and circle the one that wasn't the same. Later, *Sesame Street* brought the fun to TV with a song of encouragement. Now, almost daily, I see a screen of numbers or letters and the caption, "It will take a genius..." to figure out, for example, which one of the numbers is an 8 instead of a 9. I'm thinking it doesn't take a genius to know that you are not a genius just because you spot the one that is different.

I've seen two things in the last week that stood out from the norm and were obviously different. First, I was walking the dog one night and heard a rumbling sound as we walked down the driveway that I couldn't identify. Even the dog was looking around to see what it was. I looked up at the bright twinkling stars and clear sky and couldn't see anything that would be making the noise.

I walked the dog up the driveway, turned around, and headed back toward the highway. All of a sudden, a low hanging cloud moved swiftly across the sky. The odd shaped cloud barely cleared the apple tree in our yard. At first I thought it was smoke, but I couldn't smell it and there seemed to be no origin. To be honest, it looked creepy and when I turned my back on it to head toward the house, I felt prickles run across my scalp and had the feeling someone was watching me.

The next odd thing I saw was at the Veterans Cemetery when my son, sister-in-law, and I took flowers to place in front of Jim's niche. After we placed the flowers, we enjoyed the peaceful beauty of the cemetery. Rob and I walked away from the columbarium toward the headstones. There, not too far from the road, but several feet from the graves, was a vase of artificial flowers with a partially deflated helium balloon attached. It was stuck in the ground and looked pretty much like a fancy lawn dart. We speculated as to why the floral arrangement was in such an odd place. They weren't the same as all the other flowers placed on the graves.

We sometimes see an anomaly among our fellow human beings. Some people are just different from the others. Since we are all unique, a certain amount of difference is expected.

Jim was one of those rare individuals who marched to his own drum, and did not believe in blindly following the norm. His ideas and beliefs were often delightfully imaginative, and at the same time, his stubbornness could be maddening.

Life can become so mundane and routine that we tend to expect sameness and may not notice when things are unusual. Still, the day Jim forgot his social security number and birth date was the day I realized something was different and that nothing would ever be the same. Later, I tried to remember other clues that indicated the horrible disease that was just beginning to unfold. I couldn't think of anything that seemed to be outside the norm. Once alerted, I began to notice glitches in his thinking, his abilities, and his personality. The differences seemed to snowball, steadily going downhill and picking up speed.

It was nearly a year before others began to notice Jim's problems. Up until then, I think they believed I was exaggerating, or that *I* was the one with a problem.

Yes, we often see things that are different, but instead of really noticing them, they blend in with the minutiae of everyday life. Some differences that come out of a clear blue sky, or are stuck into a grassy knoll, make no impact on the grand scheme of things. But differences that occur in the 100 billion brain cells of someone you love are life changing.

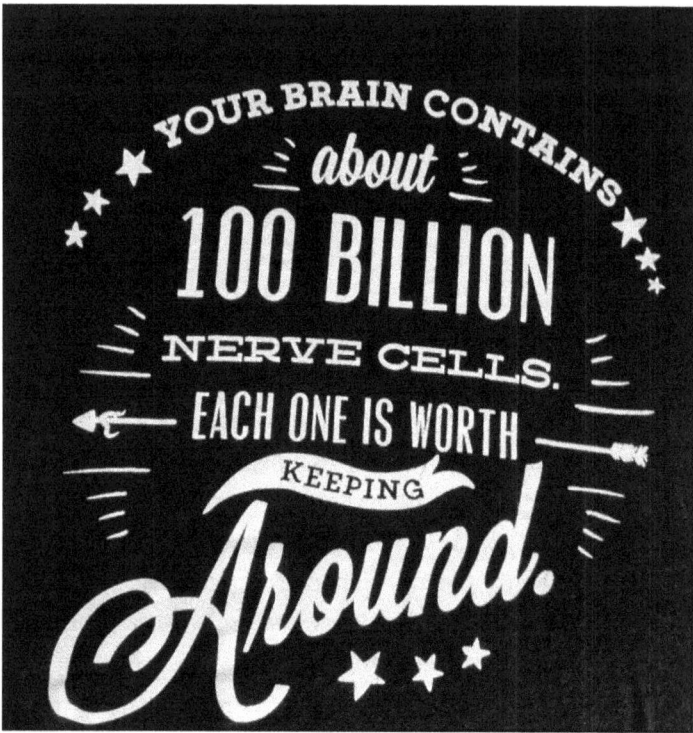

YOUR BRAIN CONTAINS about 100 BILLION NERVE CELLS. EACH ONE IS WORTH KEEPING Around.

FROM THE DAY JIM was diagnosed with an Alzheimer's type of dementia, I researched the disease through all sources possible. I used the Internet, books, pamphlets, watched TV specials, and talked to some of the top researchers in the country.

My conclusion was that early onset dementia and dementia in older people seemed to be two different diseases. It seemed obvious to me that early onset progressed much faster. That didn't seem logical since younger people generally started out with healthier bodies. Yet, I found that the median life expectancy of younger-onset Alzheimer's was six to eight years. For those diagnosed with Alzheimer's later in life, the average life expectancy was ten years, but could be as long as twenty years or more.

Now, researchers have discovered that some seniors who had been diagnosed with Alzheimer's actually had a type of dementia identified as LATE (Limbic-predominant Age-related TDP-43 Encephalopathy).

Although LATE mimics Alzheimer's disease, the proteins beta-amyloid plaques and tau tangles that are the hallmark signs of Alzheimer's do not cause the dementia. LATE is caused by deposits of the protein TDP-43 (transactive response DNA binding protein of 43 kDa) in the brain.

The report identifying LATE was published in the April 30, 2019, issue of the journal *Brain*. This is a major breakthrough in how researchers will look at dementia in older adults. LATE is believed to affect 25% of seniors with dementia who are eighty-five years or older.

At the Alzheimer's Advocacy Forum in Washington, D.C., advocates often receive reports from Richard Hodes, M.D. director of the National Institute on Aging (NIA), part of the National Institutes of Health (NIH). This latest development in the study of dementia can be seen as an opportunity. Dr. Hodes said, "The guidance provided in this report, including the definition of LATE, is a crucial step toward increasing awareness and advancing research for both this disease and Alzheimer's as well."

Abnormal TDP-3 had been previously identified in ALS (amyotrophic lateral sclerosis) also known as Lou

Gehrig's disease. TDP-3 has been found in FTLD (frontotemporal lobar degeneration). FTLD is a group of disorders that affects the frontal and/or temporal areas of the brain. FTD (frontotemporal degeneration) is a rare disease more commonly found in those younger than sixty years of age.

The progression of LATE is slower than Alzheimer's disease. When LATE and Alzheimer's disease are both present, the disease progresses more rapidly than either disease does alone.

The information from this study came from brain autopsy reports. We had an autopsy on Jim's brain for the simple reason that I wanted to know what disease he had and whether it was hereditary. Of several terms used in his autopsy, I recognized a few: *neurodegenerative* disorder, incidental *Lewy body*, *frontotemporal atrophy*, swollen *neurons*, and *tau* positive glial inclusions. The cover letter said that Jim showed no signs of Alzheimer's. He had corticobasal degeneration, a rare (non-hereditary) disease, and one I had never heard of.

Treatments targeting beta amyloid plaques would not be effective in a disease that does not have the plaques. Rare diseases do not have the funding of diseases that are more common. Funding Alzheimer's research is our greatest hope of finding effective treatment for other types of dementia.

Sources:

https://www.nia.nih.gov/news/guidelines-proposed-newly-defined-alzheimers-brain-disorder

https://www.sciencedaily.com/releases/2019/04/190430121800.htm

LOVE IS ACTION

THINKING BACK, I CAN'T remember how many weddings I've attended. The last one, just a few days ago, was for my granddaughter, Whitney. During the ceremony, the minister said something that resonated with me. He read the standard verses from 1 Corinthians 13:4-8 that I had heard at numerous weddings. After he read the verses, he pointed out that love is described as actions, not emotions.

After the promises and commitment to a life together, I watched my beautiful granddaughter dance with her handsome groom. My eyes blurred with tears at how quickly the years have gone by. I thought of her first "wedding dance" when she was curled in her Grandpa Jim's arm as she danced between us at her Uncle Bob and Aunt Stacey's wedding.

The minister's words about love being actions made me realize a truth. No matter how much someone professes their love, if their actions don't reinforce their words, they undermine them. Too often emotions stand in the way of logic, self-respect, and in extreme cases— personal safety.

Thinking of love as action is an excellent way to begin a marriage and when the time or circumstances warrant, it is the only way to end a lifetime commitment. Love as action is the best way to describe the love of a caregiver for a spouse or other family member who has dementia.

Love is patient. A caregiver has to be patient and allow her loved one to do as much as he can for as long as he can. Yes, it might be easier and faster to do it yourself, but allow extra time for your loved one to perform daily tasks. As the disease progresses, it takes time and patience to provide the level of care that a person with dementia requires.

Love is kind. As a person loses his skills, it is important to appreciate what remains instead of complaining about what a person cannot do. To belittle a person who has dementia when they make a mistake would make as much sense as kicking someone's broken leg because they couldn't walk on it. Being kind will help you sleep better at night.

It is not easily angered. When a caregiver actively cultivates patience and kindness, it would follow that he would be less likely to become angry with his loved one. You may have to constantly remind yourself that it is the disease that is responsible for behavior problems.

It always protects. One of the main jobs of a caregiver is to protect your loved one. You are responsible for your loved ones safety and physical wellbeing. You may even be responsible for your loved one's financial stability. A caregiver finds the strength to stand up against anyone who tries to take advantage or abuse her loved one in any way.

Love always hopes. When we can no longer hope for our loved one to regain his health, we can hope that he will have a good day. We can hope for a cure, so that a disease that stripped away our loved one's talents, his quality of life, or her memories won't strike others down.

Love perseveres. Dementia is not a sprint; it's a marathon. A caregiver must have perseverance to provide loving care for years and years.

Love never fails. Unconditional love is about the only way to describe caregiver love. We all expect the love we give to be reciprocated, but when dementia is involved, that may not be the case. When it comes to dementia, a parent or a spouse may become like a child. Instead of fading away, your love may become stronger as it evolves into a different kind of love—one that is action combined with the emotional memory you hold in your heart.

REUNIONS

FOR THE PAST COUPLE of years, several of us women who graduated from the same high school have met for lunch once a month. I reconnected with several friends that I hadn't seen in years. We've bonded over life's circumstances and decided that we like each other much better now that we're older. These mini reunions led to us becoming a planning committee for our 50th class reunion.

When we think about it, life is full of reunions. A chance meeting in a grocery store, a club meeting, a conference, or a public event can be a reunion. Each year at the Walk to End Alzheimer's I see some people I haven't seen in quite awhile. Some return year after year, and others are just beginning the Alzheimer's journey. These are bittersweet reunions. We are happy to see each other, sad for the circumstances.

Each year at the Alzheimer's Forum, I have a reunion with my good friends Sarah, Jane, and Kathy. A year is a long time, but it seems that we can almost pick up our conversations from the previous year mid-sentence. We all lost our husbands to dementia and developed an amazingly strong bond. We are sisters of the heart.

We reunite with friends and relatives on social media and make new "friends." We can keep up with births, deaths, marriages, as well as, what someone had for dinner. The important events are often interspersed with mundane observations, political rants, and too much information. The jury is still out as to whether the benefits outweigh the drawbacks.

We are caught up in our own little world and are shocked when we learn of a friend or family member's death. What is the first thing we all say when we run into family members at funerals? "We need to get together somewhere besides a funeral!" Sound familiar? Yet, we go our separate ways and lead our separate lives. We never get around to making that call, meeting for lunch, or making that road trip.

Since I've joined the Capps Family Band, I spend more time with my birth family than I have in years. Although I've not accomplished many of my retirement goals, at least I've done well in spending more time with my mom and siblings. We have two practice sessions a month and play music at three different nursing homes around the middle of each month.

An additional benefit of playing music is that I get to spend more time with my aunt. She likes to hear us sing at the nursing home, so my mom and I pick her up when we play in Versailles. I think I've spent more time with her in the past two years than all the years before.

Whether it's at the grocery store, a family reunion, or a chance meeting, I love running into friends and family. Even if we only have a brief conversation and a quick hug, it reminds me of the connections I've made throughout my life. Mini reunions make my heart sing.

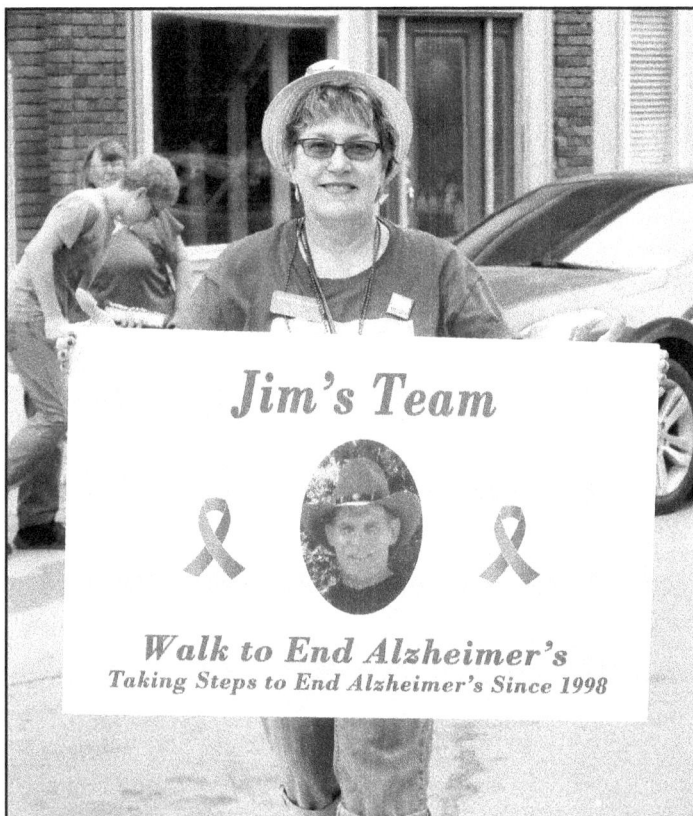

Jim's Team

Walk to End Alzheimer's
Taking Steps to End Alzheimer's Since 1998

OUR WALK TO END Alzheimer's group participated in the annual 4th of July Parade. My friend WyAnn had prepared a sign that said, *Imagine a Land Free from Alzheimer's.* Along the parade route, there isn't much time to think of anything, but after the excitement died down, I couldn't stop thinking about that sign.

What if our land was free from Alzheimer's? Think of how much that would impact the 5.8 million American families who have a loved one with

Alzheimer's disease. Imagine what a wonderful world this would be.

Our memories, personalities, and skills are the most basic part of our lives. Yet, dementia steals those precious qualities from people we love. Our mothers become our daughters. Our fathers become our sons. Our spouses become our children as we love them and care for them. Collectively, we American families provide 18.5 billion hours each year taking care of our own.

From personal experience, I can tell you that being a primary caregiver for someone with dementia is not for sissies or the squeamish. In the early stages, my caregiver duty was to keep Jim on track. I went to the doctor with him and kept track of his medication. His skill levels began to diminish. A man who once had the ability to tear a car down and put it back together would dismantle a vacuum sweeper or a VCR, but couldn't reassemble the parts.

In the middle stages, caregiving was more intense. The day started with helping him bathe and get dressed for the day. These jobs became harder as the disease progressed, and he needed more help with toileting and incontinence. Jim only needed about four hours sleep, and I couldn't sleep with him wandering around the house, or worse yet, outside in the dark. His wandering was dangerous and along with other behavior problems, it was obvious he needed a safer environment.

Caregiving doesn't end at the nursing home door! Some caregivers are comfortable with providing emotional support, interacting with staff, and supervising care. My comfort level was to make sure

Jim was clean, fed, and comfortable. For the five years Jim was in nursing care, I, or a member of our family, checked on him almost every day and assisted with his care.

The clock is ticking. Every 65 seconds another person in our land begins the Alzheimer's journey. Imagine if that didn't happen, or if it did, it could be cured. Well, if wishing and hoping could make it happen, dementia wouldn't exist.

According to the Alzheimer's Association, Alzheimer's will triple in a generation if we don't have a medical breakthrough. We can't have a breakthrough without research. When I first went to DC to advocate for Alzheimer's research funding, NIH had budgeted less than $500 million for research. I know that to you and me that sounds like a lot of money, but it is barely a blip on the radar of research possibilities. Research was stalled at a time when it should have been accelerated. If you don't see that, look at how our country used the necessary resources to find an effective treatment for HIV and AIDS. HIV/AIDS was once the inevitable death sentence that Alzheimer's is today.

It has taken us two decades to reach a level of research funding that could bring about a positive result. Now, we need to be relentless in advocating for research dollars. We cannot afford to wait another two decades for a cure. The clock is ticking.

Imagine if our land was free from Alzheimer's disease.

SHIELD FOR ALZHEIMER'S

IT IS HARD NOT to be frustrated that Alzheimer's is a terminal disease. It is easy to feel helpless and hopeless, but that is not productive. We need to grasp the reins and do everything within our power to take care of those who have the disease, find effective treatment, and find a cure. It is also a major goal to prevent Alzheimer's. Until an immunization is perfected, research has given us tools to reduce our chances of developing Alzheimer's, or possibly delay the onset.

Dr. Rudi Tanzi recommends lifestyle changes to reduce the risk of Alzheimer's disease as much as 60%. He says the word *shield* can be used to remind you of healthy habits that can benefit your body and brain.

Sleep. We need our zzz's to function. The rule of thumb used to be eight hours, but in today's world, we don't go to bed at dark and get up at daylight. Shift workers may have a difficult time to get a good "day's" sleep. When our internal circadian clock gets out of whack (not the medical term!) the brain doesn't go through its cycle to wash away the plagues that want to clog up our brains.

Handle stress. I don't want to cause stress by mentioning how detrimental to a person's health stress is. Stress releases the hormone cortisol, which can damage brain cells and cause inflammation. Recent studies indicate that brain inflammation is linked to Alzheimer's disease. We can't avoid stress; we can only manage it.

Interact with friends. Being socially active is your "friend" when fighting Alzheimer's disease. By socially, I'm not talking Facebook friends who may be more annoying than helpful. I'm talking about friends who have your back and bring joy into your life. If that happens to be your Facebook friends, then by all means, interact to your heart's content. Loneliness and isolation increases the risk of developing Alzheimer's disease.

Exercise. We all know the benefits of exercise. Exercise increases energy level, reduces stress, and helps us maintain a healthier body and brain. Yes, exercise helps your brain. It increases the blood flow in the brain and helps cognition. Find an activity you enjoy that fits your physical condition. Exercise with friends to double your fight against Alzheimer's disease!

Learn new things. If you are like me, you want to learn new things. I learned to play the ukulele about two years ago and now I've joined the family band. Learning creates new synapses in your brain. How cool is that? Having fun and helping your brain.

Diet. No, don't go on a crash diet! Yo-yo dieting is bad, bad, bad for your health. Your mama knew what she was talking about when she told you to eat your veggies. A Mediterranean type diet reduces the risk of Alzheimer's disease. A diet rich in vegetables, fruits, legumes, whole grains, fish, and olive oil is good for your heart and your brain. So, instead of starving yourself, feed your brain!

If you do all these things are you guaranteed not to develop Alzheimer's? The short answer is no. If you wear a seatbelt, it does not guarantee that you will not be injured or killed in an auto accident, but it does increase your chances of survival. If you exercise and lower cholesterol, it doesn't mean you will not have heart disease, but it lowers your risk.

Life doesn't come with a guarantee warding off ugly diseases, but use your SHIELD for the best defense against Alzheimer's disease.

Source:

Tanzi, Dr. Rudi, NBC Nightly News, July 16, 2019

https://www.youtube.com/watch?v=bgkJWQkngAw

NOT ITS INTENDED USE

A FEW YEARS AGO, we received a microwave popcorn popper as a door prize at an annual meeting. The first time we tried to pop corn, the top melted and the popcorn was charred. Since it didn't work, I prepared to dump it in the trash.

"Keep it," my husband, the farmer, said. "We might be able to use it for something else." I threw away the melted lid and kept the bottom part, against my better judgment. I saw the plastic bowl with a handle as a waste of space. Even as a popcorn popper, I didn't see much use for it since I can't eat popcorn.

Oddly enough, we use the plastic bowl almost daily for scraps and vegetable peelings. When we start preparing a meal, one of us will say, "I need the plastic bowl." Although not its intended use, it is our most used kitchen container.

Every Memorial Day, I search for a plastic vase to take fresh flowers to the Veterans Cemetery. For the unaware, it is practically impossible to find a plastic vase. My husband came up with the idea of cutting the top off a Simply Apple juice bottle and wrapping it in patriotic duck tape. Not its intended use, but it works.

Sometimes medication can be used for a different purpose, called off-label use. It takes years to develop and test medication, but when a drug can be used for more than one condition, it dramatically shortens the time to get the drug to consumers.

One of the off-label uses for the Alzheimer's drug Memantine (Nameda) is for it to be added to the standard therapy used to treat obsessive-compulsive disorder (OCD) and attention deficit order (ADHD).

Antipsychotic drugs are often used off label to treat the symptoms of Alzheimer's. One of the common drugs used is Seroquel. Another off label use for Seroquel is for insomnia.

I believe more caution should be used in prescribing antipsychotic drugs to people with Alzheimer's. Jim had some serious reactions to them. Seroquel was commonly prescribed to residents in the Alzheimer's unit. They tried it on Jim and instead of calming him, it made him hyperactive. Other psychotic drugs caused him to be angry and out of control. One even caused so much foam coming out of his mouth that he couldn't eat or drink. The physicians treating him swore they had never seen that reaction before.

Although commonly used in people with dementia, antipsychotics increase the risk of death and decrease the quality of life. While looking for a home for Jim, I visited one home where the Alzheimer's residents appeared to be in a stupor. I thought it odd at the time, but after seeing how antipsychotic drugs affect most people with dementia, I'm sure they were overmedicated.

Not all drugs used off-label are bad. Many years go into the development of prescription drugs and off-label use of an approved drug can bring relief to a patient, or even be life-saving. For example, some cancer drugs are approved for one type of cancer, but may successfully treat a different type. Chemotherapy treatments are often a combination of drugs that fight more than one type of cancer.

Sometimes, veering from the intended purpose can be successful, and sometimes it can create problems. Antipsychotic drugs for people with dementia can be life-threatening and more harmful than helpful. Using a popcorn popper for a receptacle for scraps is handy and safe—in fact, safer than using it in the microwave!

COME HOME

EACH YEAR THE MISSOURI State Fair has a theme, and this year's theme "Come Home" is thought provoking. Since I live a few short miles from the State Fair City, I just need to drive across town to "come home" to the fair.

Like many people in Sedalia, I'm not that thrilled about the fair. Oh, yes, I've enjoyed concerts, walking through the exhibits, working at the Missouri Co-op Building, and have spent countless hours on the midway while I kept an eye on the young ones in the family. I have great memories, good memories, and wish-I-was-home-under-the-air-conditioner memories.

The first night of the fair this year was pleasant, but I was too exhausted to consider going. Since then, the weather has ranged from hot to bake-a-cake hot. Then, there's the occasional thunderstorm. Oh, yes, we can be in the middle of a drought, but you can count on rain during the fair.

One of the first things that crossed my mind with "Come Home" was the exact feeling I always had when Jim and I drove into Estes Park. We went to Rocky Mountain National Park each year, and although some things changed from year-to-year, the predominant emotion was a sense of homecoming.

Along with the eventual changes in Estes Park were the inevitable changes in Jim. Our first trips, we spent camping, hiking, and going to the Lazy-B Ranch for music and a delicious meal. The last few times, we stayed in a cabin, and I watched Jim lose the ability to camp and hike. It was the end of an era for us.

While Jim was in the nursing home, I made a trip to Estes Park with my mom, sister, and sister-in-law. I hadn't been to the mountains for several years. It was like coming home to a different house. Everything had changed so much physically and emotionally. Several of my favorite shops had closed, the visitor's center had grown into a huge hub of activity, and the Lazy-B Ranch was no longer in existence. I didn't have Jim to cook a campfire breakfast, to sneak treats to "Chubby" the chipmunk, or to sit around the campfire and tell tall tales.

We all know that everything changes through the years, even our home. We may long for the familiar home of our memories and to see loved ones who live in the homes of our hearts, but are no longer with us.

Home is where our stories began and where we became who we are. It doesn't matter if we lived in a shack long ago and now live in a mansion. There is a chunk of our being that is wrapped in the recollections of our beginnings.

Home. The word isn't just any old word. Home is a word that entails a visual image in 3-D, complete with smells and sounds. Memories of home can be good or bad for a lot of reasons. Regardless, it is a big part of each of us. The lessons we learn from our parents mingle with our DNA to mold us into the adults we become later in life.

Into Each Life

On this cloudy, rainy August day, I thought about the Henry Wadsworth Longfellow quote, "Into each life, some rain must fall." It seems that sometimes the rain falls harder than it does at other times.

Last year, our Walk to End Alzheimer's was during a steady downpour. We had rain at previous walks, but never a constant deluge like last year. Although the Highway Gardens at the Missouri State Fairgrounds is a lovely place to hold our walk, the grounds turned into a mud pit. Tents and tables sank into the mud and turned over. I couldn't take my books out of the tubs.

Although, we handled the weather as well as could be expected, it inspired us to get off our keisters and look for a location that had some shelter. This year, for the first time, we chose Centennial Park and a different weekend.

When you hold an annual outdoor event, it isn't a matter of *if* it will rain on that special day, but *when* it will rain. The same holds true for life. Rain happens.

Gully washers happen during our darkest moments. We hear the rolling thunder and feel sharp pangs of lightning bolts when they strike our hearts. Clouds seem to hang over our heads blocking out the sunshine that should warm our souls. Flash floods threaten to wash away our optimism and feelings of self worth.

Sometimes, we have steady downpours. Just when we think we're between showers, it starts up again soaking us to the bone. Then, a cold wind blows away our defenses, and we might as well be naked as wrapped in wet garments. We get to the point where we just can't take anymore. At some point, a little droplet of rain can be the tipping point.

During scattered showers, we can dash from thought to action and never get wet. If all fails, we can throw on a rain jacket and pop up an umbrella. We know that scattered showers replenish our spirits and blossoms into a bright array of color. During scattered showers, we realize that rain is essential to life and that without it, we, and everything we love, would die. Then the sun breaks through the clouds and we remember that "a sunshiny shower won't last half an hour."

A half hour isn't long and most of us can remain optimistic for that length of time. Life is different degrees of rain, but rain is essential to life.

CAR CONVERSATIONS

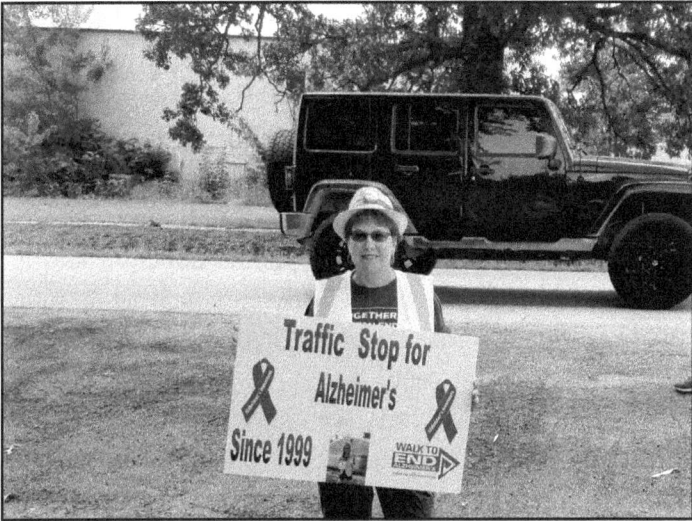

WE HAD OUR ANNUAL Walk to End Alzheimer's fundraising "Traffic Stop" on Labor Day. As usual, the day had its busy times and its lulls. Our collections depend on the traffic building up at the stop sign in my hometown.

We took our positions along the road with our collection buckets. My granddaughter entertained with her purple flag. She threw it in the air and after it whirled around, she caught it, whipping into a pose. Several people applauded, others cheered, and some commented on how impressive she was.

"You are helping my collections," I told her. I commented on her poses after she caught it.

"I'm not showing off," she said. "I went down on my knee because that's how I was able to catch the flag." She laughed and tossed it high. "If I wanted to show off," she said, "I would do this." She caught the flag and did the splits.

This year, the city police officer decided to direct traffic—to avoid the backlog. This has only happened a couple of times in the 21 years we've collected. As the traffic approached us, the officer stood in the intersection, gesturing for the cars to keep moving.

One lady stopped in front of me, ignoring the urgency of the officer. She dropped a donation into the container I held out for her. With tears welling up in her eyes, she said, "My husband died from Alzheimer's about this time last year."

With those few words, we connected. "I'm so sorry. I lost my husband to dementia too," I said. She paused a moment, as if she had much more to say but couldn't find the words. Then she drove through the intersection.

"He isn't doing us any favors," I told my sister. "It's a little hard to collect when the traffic is whizzing by." At least he wasn't there all the time. He would leave and return periodically.

Car after car ignored the opportunity to go through the intersection as they paused to give us collections and share their stories. My granddaughter said, "The officer underestimated the generosity of people."

The cool morning turned into a warm afternoon. We had mini-conversations with the donors. One woman handed me a $20 bill. "This is to honor my mom and my grandma. They both have Alzheimer's."

After each donation, I said, "Thank you, have a safe trip home." Several people automatically said, "You too." Some of them seemed to hesitate as they realized they had wished me a safe trip. One woman seemed particularly frustrated that she had said it. I laughed. "Everyone says the same thing," I assured her.

One man told me, "I don't have any money, but I'm going to the bank. I'll be back," he promised.

The day wore on. I heard stories about moms, dads, sisters, brothers, and friends who were living with dementia or had died with it.

The officer had left the intersection and we saw his car on a side street. We assumed he was keeping an eye on the traffic from the comfort of his car rather than standing in the middle of a hot street. We heard a siren. He pulled a car over in front of where my daughter-in-law Stacey was collecting. After he finished writing the ticket and walked back to his patrol car, I saw a hand come out the window to give Stacey a donation.

The afternoon sun was beating mercilessly down on us, so we began to gather up the signs and pinwheels. A car drove onto the side street behind us and the driver handed Stacey a $20 bill.

After he drove off, she turned to me and said, "That man told me he had to go to the bank."

"He told me the same thing! I never really thought he meant it," I said.

I guess you just can't underestimate the generosity of people.

TIME TO RUMINATE

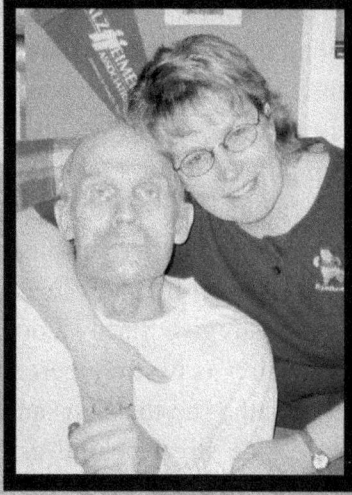

LIFE HAS BEEN SO hectic the past few weeks that I haven't had time for a fleeting thought, much less rumination. If I could only find a way to add more hours to the day, it would be helpful.

I guess in a way, I *have* added more hours. Unfortunately, the hours are stolen from sleep time. I've been in the bad habit of going to bed at midnight and due to appointments, conferences, Walk to End

Alzheimer's, etc, etc, I've been getting up early, earlier, or earliest.

Lately, if I can't find two things to do at once, I feel like I'm wasting precious time. I watch TV and play games on my Kindle at the same time. I walk the dog and practice songs for our nursing home gigs. I stop on my way to the basement to play a short song on my ukulele. You get the idea, I'm sure.

Of course, this doubling up can cause chaos at times. I spilled milk two days in a row—once on my PC and the other time all over the counter and (oops) my husband. Occasionally, I put something in the cabinet that should have gone in the refrigerator, or leave my phone in the living room and pick up the TV remote instead.

Last week, my husband and I mowed our acres of lawn, and I had some quality rumination time while I mowed. Although I was exhausted, I decided to use the trimmer, but the battery was dead. (Darn the luck!) I put the battery on the charger, took a shower, and a nap.

The next day, I tackled the weeds around our bevy of hydrants. As I was starting to wear down, I looked at my cell phone to see how long I'd been at it. As I pulled the phone out of my pocket, it began to play a Carter family song from the early 1950s "It's My Lazy Day." Seriously? Is that irony, or what? My smart phone is a smart-aleck phone.

After I finished with the yard work, I put Walk to End Alzheimer's signs and some of the pinwheel flowers from previous walks in our yard. Once I went inside, I signed copies of "Ruminations of a Caregiver" to hand out at Saturday's Walk to End Alzheimer's.

While I was frantically trying to get everything done, I was home alone when I started having chest pains. Yes, I've had them before, and had three stress tests that showed my heart was in A-1 shape. I took the meds that should have stopped the pain, but it kept right on coming. I was 99% sure it was nothing to worry about, but that bitty 1% warned that my pain was classic heart attack symptoms. All I have to say is never think you might be having a heart attack without taking a book to read. I spent the better part of the day being poked and prodded, just to reaffirm that I had a non-emergency, emergency.

Anyway, the Walk to End Alzheimer's was a resounding success this year. We had beautiful weather, great attendance, and exceeded our goal. So Saturday was a long day, but a fulfilling day.

Whew. Finally, I felt like I could rest, except Sunday was music practice; Monday, a doctor's appointment; and Tuesday, advocacy training; Wednesday, we played music at the first of three nursing homes.

Thursday, I had my oil changed, tires rotated, and brakes worked on. It was time well spent because I logged on to the wi-fi and played my game while I waited. Soon, I was speeding down the road, listening to music on Sirius FM. I switched between stations listening for songs I might want to sing. Music is soul food and conducive to rumination.

LIFE IS A MIST

SOMETIMES I HEAR A MESSAGE on Sunday morning that speaks to my heart. This Sunday, Associate Pastor Candice talked about the book of James. The gist of the section was we should not brag about tomorrow because we don't know what tomorrow might bring. I underlined, "You are a mist that appears for a little while and then vanishes."

This really puts into perspective how fleeting life is and what a small speck our years here on earth are in the realm of eternity. So what do we do with our precious time? We fight. We argue. We worry about tomorrow. We think of ourselves as important—at least in our own little corner of the world.

When I was a little girl, I sometimes wondered if people existed when they weren't where I could see them. Talk about thinking I was the center of the world!

I don't know at what point in my life I stopped those foolish thoughts. At least I was a kid. I know people who think the world revolves around them and they are supposedly all grown up.

The thought that life is but a mist really fits into my line of thought now. As Dorothy said when she was in OZ, "My! People come and go so quickly here." If you think about the people in your life, you will see that like the mist, they sometimes surround you with love and other times they vanish into thin air.

We lose people for a lot of reasons. Often, the reason is indifference. They no longer play a relevant part in our lives, and we let them slip away into the mist of the forgotten. Sometimes, the reason is distance. Separation can be caused by miles and miles of physical distance, or by the distance of growing apart philosophically or simply from having nothing in common.

Other people we love regardless of how far adrift they are from our everyday lives. Family ties can transcend any barriers. Friends are the family we choose. True friends can practically pick up in the middle of a conversation although they may have not seen each other for months.

When we are separated from our loved ones by death, sometimes we can feel their presence and at times reach out to touch them in our minds, hearts, and dreams. They are gone, but they are here in a way that can comfort us. Memories can hit with such force that it takes our breath away. The mist clears and we find ourselves in another moment, another time, a different dimension.

Life is a mist. What is important? I remember one time a woman asked me if I was jealous of my sister because she lived in a new, lovely home. At the time, Jim and I were renting an old house with sloping floors and ill-fitting windows. We had old furniture we'd bought from a second hand store. Still, I thought it sounded like a ridiculous idea. "No," I said. "I'm happy for her." And I meant it. I had zero jealousy or envy.

What is important to me is not to be famous, rich, or have my name remembered by strangers. I have no desire to be important in worldly ways. All I want is to fulfill the mission I've been given in life. I want to give more than I take. I want to love and to be loved.

I want to know the good I can do and then do it. I don't want to do it for outward recognition; I want to do it for the way it makes me feel on the inside.

When my mist vanishes, I want my legacy to be a life well lived, and more importantly, a life well loved.

IF YOU THINK YOU'RE BUSY

MY FRIEND JUDY USED to say, "If you think you're busy now—retire." At the time, I was working full time, taking care of Jim, volunteering for the Alzheimer's Association, and involved in Writers' Guild. I thought there was no way that I could possibly be any busier.

Fast forward to now and I don't know how I ever had time to work. It seems that life should be more laid back in retirement, and I should have plenty of time to read and relax. Except that I don't. Reading is usually reserved for bedtime, unless I get to feeling feisty and spend the entire day in my pj's curled up with a book. Well, I'm sure that's happened at least once since I retired in 2013.

I saw a post a few days ago that said something about instead of making a to-do list, make a to-be list. It went on to list things that a person might want to be. Of course, I can't find where I saw it, so the absolute queen of the to-do list—actually multitasking by having several lists going at the same time—I decided to work on my own to-be list.

Some of the things I want to be:

Happy. I'm not talking about telling a joke happy, because even the most depressed people may laugh the loudest at a joke. I want to feel happiness in my soul, in my being. I want to wake up each day to the thought that each day gives me new opportunities to achieve my life's goals. Each day gives me a chance to let go of yesterday's problems or failures.

Appreciative. I want always to be grateful for time spent with family and friends. I appreciate that my health, although not perfect, allows me to do most of the things I want to do. Sure, it hurts my fingers to type, but I can still work for a while before they quit on me. I want to concentrate on what's working instead of what's gone wrong.

Thoughtful. Being thoughtful is a two-sided coin. One side is to be thoughtful of others and never hurt someone's feelings deliberately. The other side is that I want to think things through before popping off with something that offends others. I want to think for myself, not be influenced by someone's outrage or political agenda. I hope that I'm always capable of being introspective and never have a disease that would take that away from me.

A Good Judge of Character. I want to surround myself with honest, moral humans. I realize that no one is perfect and they won't always agree with me (even when I'm right), but if they have my back, I'll have theirs. I can forgive a lot of flaws, but I don't want to waste my time with liars, cheaters, thieves, or con artists.

Able to Laugh. I have some family and friends who have no sense of humor. Laughter is good for my mental health. If I can laugh at myself when I make silly mistakes, it helps me to forgive myself for moments of stupidity.

A Woman Who Always Makes the Most of Life. I don't just want to be alive—I want to live. I realize that time manages me more than I manage it. I have books to read, places to go, things to do, books to write, and songs to sing.

Yes, I'm busier than a normal human being should be, but it's the lifestyle I've chosen. I may want long "to-do" lists of tasks, but my "to-be" list stretches to infinity and beyond.

LITTLE THINGS

OUR SEDALIA BUSINESS WOMEN'S Club just finished celebrating National Business Women's week. We had an activity planned for every day except Friday. We kicked off the week with our annual fundraising chicken dinner. Monday, we had lunch with Rotary. Tuesday, we had our past president's dinner. Wednesday, we had friendship lunch. Thursday, was our membership activity with, you guessed it, heavy snacks. Saturday was a social activity with shopping and food. Sunday, was church with the president, followed with lunch at a local restaurant. I'm pleased to announce that somehow I only gained one pound.

Our club begins each monthly dinner meeting with the Club Collect. Often, when you recite a poem, or in this case, a prayer, you don't always ponder the meaning behind the words.

From beginning to end, the Collect for Club Women is chock-full of wisdom. The part that has been on my mind lately is the sentence: "Grant that we may realize it is the little things that create differences, that in the big things of life we are at one."

Have you ever had a terrible argument with a friend or family member, and a week later, you are still upset with them but can't remember what started it? That's because you have let some small insignificant disagreement cause a big uproar.

One time when I had to have surgery, Jim was much more worried about it than I was. Since I had to stay in the hospital a few days, I wanted a new robe and house shoes to match. Finally, in frustration he shouted at me, "You seem to be more worried about matching your outfit than you are about the surgery!" Actually, I was covering up my nervousness by concentrating more on the little things that apparently we disagreed on, than the big thing like being knocked out while the surgeon ripped out body parts.

Later when I became Jim's caregiver, I was able to deal with big problems better than day-to-day issues. I could handle a major medical problem, but if he didn't eat his dinner, I could have a meltdown.

Little things can create differences that spill over into the big things, especially when dealing with a grudge holder. I confess that I was once a grudge holder, but somewhere along life's pathway, I discovered that grudges were a total waste of time.

Yet, I've seen life-long friendships and marriages break up over the little things. Some people can be so persnickety, that they tend to get on your nerves. Sometimes, it's just better to capitulate. Let's face it when someone wants things done a certain way, then if you don't do it to suit them enough times, they will either live with the way you do it, or do it themselves. I call that a win-win.

Other times people (for a lack of better words) seek revenge. I know a man who complained every day about the lunch his wife fixed him. One day, she had her fill of his complaints, so she put a picture of a sandwich between two pieces of bread and put it in his lunchbox. I don't know if he ever asked her to pack his lunch again.

The best plan is not let the little battles blow up into WW3. After all, differences are what makes a relationship interesting. If we all thought alike, the world would be unbearably boring.

HALLOWEEN SPIDERS

LAST WEEK SOME OF my friends and I were discussing an article in the paper about a ghost hunter in our town. "I don't know if as Christians, we should believe that ghosts exist. Do you believe in ghosts?" she asked me.

"Oh, yes," I said. I told her a quick story about a "ghost" car that Jim and I had seen on an evening walk many years ago. I didn't tell her about my many other close encounters with the unexplainable.

It always seems that at Halloween time, the weird and strange seems to be on our minds. I take special care to avoid creepy things anymore, and try not to call attention to myself when it comes to the paranormal. My brother and I wrote a book a few years ago, *Apparitions: Twisted Tales and Yarns*, which was *mostly* fiction.

Anyway, Halloween is just a fun time for me now, with all things calm and normal. I even bought a pair of Halloween leggings adorned with spider webs. I completed my outfit with a pair of spider web/spider earrings. I wore my outfit the day our family band played music for a food drive in our hometown. After we packed away our instruments and said our goodbyes, I headed home.

I was cruising along listening to Prime Country when I noticed a dark spot out of the corner of my eye. I occasionally have "floaters" and thought this was a particularly bad one. Then I noticed that it seem to be moving. I reached up, pulled off my glasses, and my floater turned out to be a spider web stuck to my glasses. I thought that was a little bit coincidental since I was wearing all my spidery garb.

A few days later, I wore the same outfit to town. As I was sitting in the left hand turn lane waiting for the light to change, I dialed my mom's number to chat with her on my way home. She answered the phone at the same moment a mean looking spider crawled across my windshield. "I have to get this spider out of my car," I said.

My mom had me on speaker and my brother and sister-in-law could hear me. My sister-in-law told me I should not be talking on the phone while I was driving—much less battling a spider. "It's hands free," I explained, as I pushed the button to lower the window. I grabbed a piece of mail off the seat and tried to flip the spider out the window.

Now why would a spider go out the window when he had a gigantic web all over my legs? Well, he disappeared all right, but I didn't know where he went. I finally made my left-hand turn and pulled into a parking lot. I jumped out frantically brushing off my clothes, shaking my hair, examining the car. He was nowhere to be found. I don't know what happened to him.

I do know that I had three people laughing at me as I cautiously crawled back into my car. I guess I couldn't just abandon my car because a darned spider was hiding out in it—somewhere.

When I think about it, the spider pants seemed to be a spider magnet. All I can say is I'm glad I chose them over the second choice—ghost pants.

IN REMEMBRANCE

AT CHURCH, I SAT behind the man who had been our family doctor until he retired in 2012. As we greeted each other, he said, "I didn't recognize you at first." That should have been my clue to tell him my name, but I didn't get a chance before we started singing. After all, we had one family doctor and he had hundreds of patients, so that didn't surprise me too much.

It was communion Sunday, and our associate pastor quoted the passage where Jesus said, "Do this in remembrance of me."

As we returned to our seats after communion, doc turned around and said, "Are you still Mrs. Fisher?"

"Yes," I said. "I remarried, but kept my name."

"I remember Jimmy," he said. "Your name is Linda, right?" I nodded. "It's a shame that you both had to go through that."

We finished services with a benediction and our final song. As we were walking out, he said, "You know, Jimmy won't look the same when we get to heaven, but we will know him."

I could feel tears welling in my eyes, and I said, "I know he will be whole again."

When I dream of Jim, he doesn't have dementia. When I think of Jim, I want to remember him as he was before dementia, and sometimes I do. Sometimes, I think of how life changed so drastically when he began forgetting how to remember. He had a phenomenal ability to recall memories, or to reminisce, as his brother Bob called it.

It is safe to say that I think of Jim every day. Sometimes, the thoughts are fleeting and other times they hit me hard. I've lost other loved ones that I think of often, but not that I think of on a daily basis.

This morning, I was going to town and had some anxious thoughts about what the day was going to bring. Then, a song came on the radio that immediately took me back to a different time. The song I was hearing, "Cinderella," made me think of Jim, strumming his guitar, and singing the song to me. He would sing, "Lindarella." The remembrance made me both sad and happy.

Throughout life, we find moments we'd just as soon forget, but those little snippets of memory can enrich our lives if we let them. It is our past that makes us who we are today. Who we are and what we do today will be tomorrow's memories, so we want to make them worthwhile.

REMEMBER, REMEMBER

WHEN I WAS A KID, someone gave us a set of the *World Book of Knowledge*. I was always looking for something to read and found the books much more interesting than the backs of cereal boxes.

Although the books were full of history, science, and various other subjects for school age children, I always started (and usually ended) with the literature section in the middle. The literature section had stories and poems. I memorized dozens of poems and one came in handy this month.

I made an appointment and recited, "Remember, remember the fifth of November." I knew I had said that twice. Unfortunately, I couldn't recall what I was going to remember. When I flipped the wall calendar to the new month, the fifth of November was a blank square. My PC was downstairs in the safe, and my phone had a dead battery.

I puzzled over the situation. I knew it was about time for my hair appointment, and sure enough when the battery came to life—there it was. This morning when I turned on my PC, I saw the other reminder. I can now get my second pneumonia shot. Well, I didn't rush into get my shot, but I kept the hair appointment.

Rhyming poetry is a good way to memorize information. It's how I used to remember how many days were in each month until I worked for more than thirty years plugging in the last day of the month for our reports. I no longer had to say, "Thirty days has September, April, June, and November…" Then there's the "i" before "e" poem, although that one is pretty worthless because of all the exceptions.

Being able to remember important events is something all of us strive to do. Life can get so busy at times, that I often think of events after it's too late. My phone does its best to remind me of everything I need to do. I even have my grocery list on it. I'm not sure how reliable my memory is without all the bells and whistles of my electronic calendars.

Being forgetful is something that concerns me. Alzheimer's scares me more than any other disease. I shudder to think that an irreversible, progressive disease could erode my skills, erase my memories, and thrust me into a world of confusion.

I can't imagine anything sadder than not recognizing my grandchildren. If I lost the ability to read or write, it would change who I am as a person.

With Jim, the thing I hated the most was that we had to place him in a Special Care Unit. He was locked inside, and it hurt my heart that he lost the freedom he had risked his life for in Vietnam. That Jim spent the last decade of his life in a faraway place is one of life's unexplained mysteries. Bad things should happen to bad people not to good people.

The "Serenity Prayer" encourages us to accept what we cannot change. I have come to realize that *what-ifs* and *could have beens* only steal my joy, and need to be banished forever. I want to change the things I can, and know that I certainly need wisdom to make that happen.

CONVERSATIONS

WHEN JIM DEVELOPED DEMENTIA, one of the things I missed the most was our conversations. No matter what the daily schedule, we always took time to drink a cup of coffee and talk. Most of the time, our first cup of coffee was in bed propped up on our pillows.

Our first indication that Jim had dementia was the day he couldn't remember his social security number or his birth date. To forget any date, much less his birth date, set off the alarms in my head.

At first, he still looked and sounded the same. As time passed, he became vague in his speech and searched for words for common objects. He often became frustrated when he couldn't communicate.

Gradually, our conversations became less meaningful until after a few years, Jim developed aphasia and became mostly nonverbal. He used what I refer to as "stock" phrases. Some of his favorites were "right here, but I can't find it" or "I have no idea" or "is that right?" and "you're going the wrong way." I saw him have conversations with strangers, and he inserted enough "is that right's" that the person had no idea that Jim had dementia.

After you are around someone with dementia, you are more attuned to the language changes that indicate an underlying neurodegenerative disorder. Subtle changes in speech may occur up to a decade before the onset of dementia, or as in Jim's case, a short time. Researchers are using speech patterns as a way to identify at risk individuals with mild cognitive impairment (MCI) and those who are in the earliest stages of dementia.

1. **Rambling and Non-specific Speech.** People with MCI may use more words than necessary when they speak. Individuals in the early stages of dementia will have trouble finding the correct words, talk in simplified sentences, and make more grammatical errors than normal. Word finding may lead to calling objects by the wrong name, for example calling an apple an "orange." It can also lead to a lengthy description instead of a word. When they can't recall the word "book," they may say, "You know, that thing with words and those things you turn…"

2. **Formulaic Speech.** Formulaic speech is a more scientific version of what I referred to earlier as Jim's "stock" phrases. Using a lot of common phrases repetitively such as "you know

what I mean" when a person cannot express what he or she is trying to say.

3. Weak Language. A person with dementia may start to speak in fragmented sentences and not finish complete thoughts. They stop using less common words and use fewer meaningful adverbs or adjectives.

4. Not Understanding Written Language. Along with speech problems, persons with cognitive problems may have trouble reading. They might be able to recite written words, or even read a book, but not fully understand what they have read. Jim was a prolific reader and we were regulars at our local independent bookstore. I began to notice that Jim sometimes bought a duplicate or triplicate of the same book. He was reading, turning the pages, but he couldn't follow the storyline.

5. Unusually Rude Speech. As language skills erode, frustration can make a person with dementia rude. If the part of the brain is damaged that filters thoughts from being spoken aloud, the brain doesn't censor what comes out of the mouth. After Jim quit smoking and stores relegated smokers to benches near the entrance of the store, Jim would shake his finger at complete strangers and say, "You better quit that damn smoking."

6. Repetitive questions. Individuals with dementia often use repetitive phrases or ask the same question multiple times. When short term memory is affected, they may not realize they are repeating themselves. As annoying as it is, it is best to validate the person with an acknowledgement they have spoken.

The stage of dementia and the type of dementia affects communication to different degrees and in different ways. It is sad that a degenerative brain disease can so adversely affect a person who was once highly intelligent and a great conversationalist.

When I watch old videotapes of Jim, I realize how much I missed his jokes, observations, and singing during the last several years of his life. But most of all, I missed our conversations over our morning coffee.

WHERE'S THE SKILLET?

I READ RECENTLY THAT everyone has a favorite burner on the stove, but don't talk about it. Not only do we have a favorite burner, we have a favorite skillet. In fact, we can't seem to fix breakfast without that skillet.

A few weeks ago, I inhaled a few cups of coffee and prepared to fix breakfast. I opened the cabinet to drag out "the" skillet, and although the shelf had other skillets, it didn't have the breakfast skillet. I picked up the larger skillets, as if the smaller one could be hiding beneath them. But no, it wasn't there. Breakfast was on hold while the search began.

It seems that more and more objects have been disappearing lately. Made me wonder if poltergeists were playing tricks on us.

Missing, missing, missing. After a thorough search of the kitchen, I found the skillet—not in the normal place, but in with the pots.

"You're losing it," my husband said. That was before he tore up his office looking for two expensive missing program discs. Which, I might add are missing to this day.

"At least it wasn't in the refrigerator," I defended myself. I remembered that misplacing items are a sign of normal aging if you find objects in a halfway logical place. If you find it in a really weird place, it could be Warning Sign #7 that you might have Alzheimer's.

I can just tick off the missing: gloves, coats, favorite shirts, sock mates, my seasonal clothing, lids for storage bowls, and just this morning a container of fruit. I had just fixed the fruit and couldn't figure out what I had done with it. After a search, I found it on the bathroom counter where I had gone to turn off hubby's razor that he left running.

OK. Now, I admit that (a) that wasn't a logical place for the container of fruit, but (b) I was able to retrace my steps. Score one for me, (a) is a sign of Alzheimer's, but (b) is normal aging. I call that a wash, wouldn't you?

I've discovered there is a rule of lost and found. All you have to do is replace an item to find the original you lost. I lost my nail clippers—well, more like several clippers—but I lost my last ones. I need to keep my nails clipped to play my ukulele. I was on my way to practice our program for the nursing homes, so I stopped at Dollar General to buy nail clippers. Of course, a few days later, I found a nice (gold plated) set of clippers in a drawer.

The lost is usually found—eventually—even if you can't retrace your steps. Last year, I could only find my ugly Christmas sweater, but this year I found the rest of them in a downstairs closet.

My husband had the serial numbers for his two programs so he was able to get electronic copies to put on his new PC. As for the original programs, maybe I should check the freezer.

FIFTY YEARS AGO

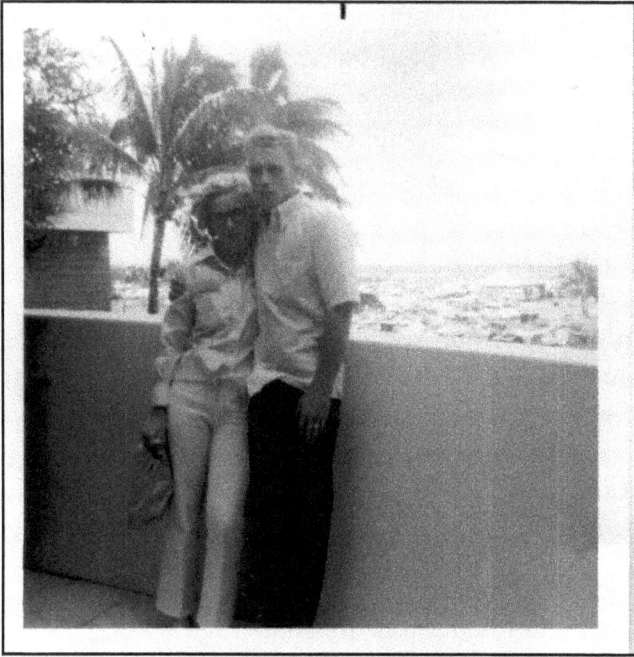

FIFTY YEARS AGO TODAY, Jim and I were married in a tiny chapel on Fort DeRussy in Honolulu, Hawaii. This whole marriage thing was quite the adventure.

Jim had been in Vietnam eight months and was due for R&R. He floated the idea that he could take R&R in Hawaii and we could get married. Once he got the approval, the only obstacle was money. I was a college student, and Jim had been sending his check to his mom and dad who were in dire financial straits.

Never to be deterred, Jim took what little money he had and won enough at a craps game to buy my ticket and reserve a hotel room at the Ilikai.

I set off to Hawaii on a cold December day after reading the book *Airport*. While waiting to board the plane I joked with my mom and dad about which of the passengers looked like a bomber. Well, the joke was on me when we made an emergency landing in Denver. Of course, they didn't even tell us we were landing, but it became obvious as the ground got closer and closer. We landed on an apparently abandoned runway being followed by fire trucks, police cars, ambulances, and taxis. After spending several hours in a hanger, they finally told us that someone had called in a bomb threat for our flight.

They put us on a different plane and sent us on our way. When our flight got to San Francisco, we flew in circles for an hour above a thunderstorm until we were cleared to land. My connecting flight was long gone. I sat in the airport for the rest of the day waiting for a plane delayed by a snowstorm in New York.

Jim and I were supposed to get married on Friday, December 19, but it was late at night before I made it to Hawaii. The next day, we took a taxi up into the mountains to get our marriage license. Except, my family doctor used a form for my blood test that had additional information on it, but he only filled out the part required in Missouri. It had all the info needed in Hawaii, but she couldn't accept an incomplete form.

Her husband drove us to a clinic in downtown Honolulu and a physician transferred the info to a Hawaiian form. Then, we went back to the mountains to get the license. Guess what? The chapel closed at noon and we couldn't make it back in time. Jim placed a phone call and used his persuasive line of gab to get the chaplain to wait for us. When we came rushing through the door at one o'clock and handed him the license, he had his employees witness our signatures and excused them to go home.

I had never dreamed of a big wedding, but I certainly never thought I'd have a wedding with three people, including the groom and me!

Fifty years ago today, started the life that was to be mine for thirty-five years. We lived in poverty for several years, but eventually had a decent income. We had ups and downs, fights, and abundant love.

We had a lot of years of "sickness" and not too many of health. I can't say I wouldn't have changed a thing, because I'd have definitely changed Jim's mental and physical health, and would have skipped the dementia part completely. Still, the family that I love dearly today is possible because a couple of kids, who against all odds, got married on this day in 1969. Smiles to heaven, Jim. I am a much better person for having known your wholehearted love and loving you to the moon and back.

RUNAWAY TRAIN OF TIME

IT'S HARD TO THINK that another year is nearing its end. I shouldn't be surprised since time seems to pass by faster and faster each day. Sometimes I feel like time is a runaway train, and I'm barely hanging onto the caboose.

On Christmas day, I was walking my dog and reflecting on Christmases past. For some reason, a memory popped up out of the blue that hadn't crossed my mind for years. I was thinking about how Jim didn't enjoy all the Christmas brouhaha. In his mind, Christmas had lost its true meaning as it became more commercialized resulting in more pressure to buy gifts.

Jim's family decided to exchange names one year, and Jim didn't want any part of it. Anyway, I participated, never suspecting what my gift was going to be. Jim's Grandpa Tubbs drew my name, and you'll have to admit the man had a sense of humor. He watched expectantly as I opened my gift. He had given me an orange, transparent negligee. I'm not sure my red face went too well with the orange!

My dog thought I was a little bit crazy when I started laughing out loud, but I found a lot of humor in remembering that unusual gift.

This time of year, we tend to reflect on the year in review—or sometimes, a lifetime in review. Each year has its challenges, tragedies, and triumphs. Families grow and families shrink. Our circle of friends and supporters may increase, or they may fade away.

Sometimes, when we are spreading the merry and bright messages, the words of cheer only serve to bring out the sadness of the holidays. For those who are missing their loved ones or have health problems, the holidays can be an endurance test. Enduring and enjoying are worlds apart.

In many ways, I'm in a better place than I was this time last year, but in other ways, this year has brought a new set of troubles. All I can say is while bad things occurred this year, I feel that if I kept score, I'd find that more good things happened.

A lot of people make resolutions this time of the year. I never found a resolution that I couldn't break within a week. If I were to look at the year ahead and decide what I would like to see change, I can think of one obvious thing. I'd like to spend more time playing and less time working. It's not unusual for me to spend an entire day without a chance to sit down—and when I sit down, I'm often at my computer working on one project or another.

A goal I set last year was to get more sleep. Well, that hasn't worked out. I stay up until midnight, day after day, and then often wake before the alarm goes off. To top it all off, if I have one good night's sleep, I have another that is restless. I believe this is a left over from the days when Jim wandered at night. The doctor finally gave him a sleeping pill, but that only worked for about four hours. Then, we were both up, Jim trying to leave, and me determined to make him stay.

Living human beings are survivors. We each have fought our own battles, suffered unbearable losses, and picked ourselves up and dusted off despair. We relegate the hurt to a special part of our brains and go about the business of surviving.

As time passes by, living life to the fullest is the best way to honor our loved ones who are no longer with us. I hope that while I hang on to the runaway train of time, I open my eyes and enjoy the glorious view for I will never pass this way again.

ALZHEIMER'S ANTHOLOGY OF
UNCONDITIONAL LOVE

Edited by L. S. Fisher

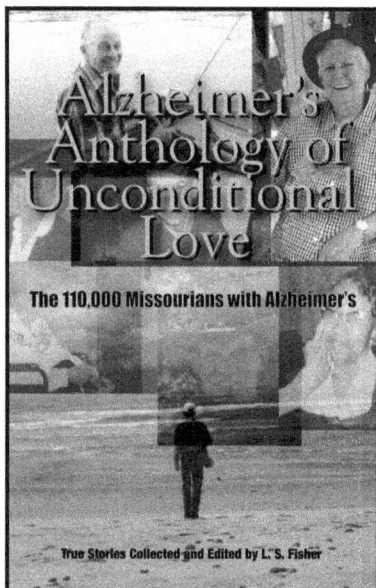

Mozark Press
PO Box 1746
Sedalia, MO 65302

www.MozarkPress.com
www.lsfisher.com

EARLY ONSET BLOG: ESSAYS FROM AN ONLINE JOURNAL

By L. S. Fisher

Mozark Press
PO Box 1746
Sedalia, MO 65302

www.MozarkPress.com
www.lsfisher.com

EARLY ONSET BLOG: THE FRIENDSHIP CONNECTION
&
OTHER ESSAYS

By L. S. Fisher

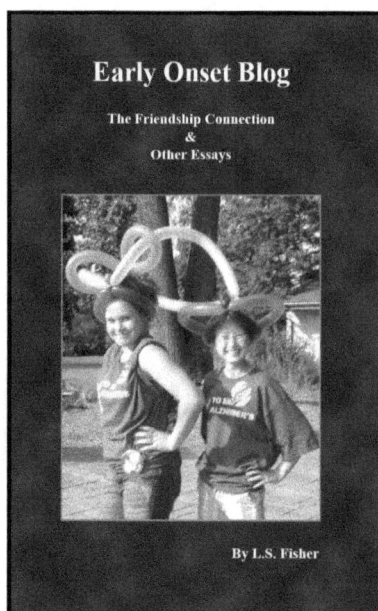

Mozark Press
PO Box 1746
Sedalia, MO 65302

www.MozarkPress.com
www.lsfisher.com

EARLY ONSET ALZHEIMER'S
ENCOURAGE, INSPIRE, AND INFORM

By L. S. Fisher

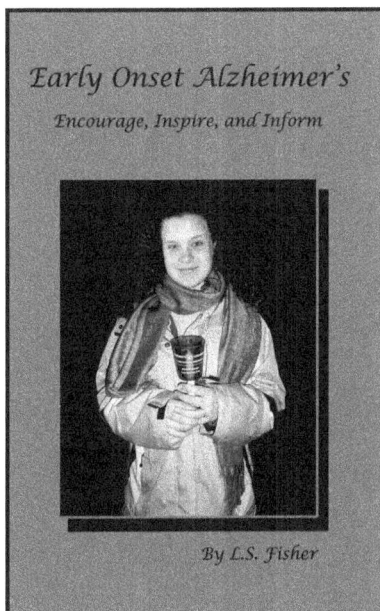

Mozark Press
PO Box 1746
Sedalia, MO 65302

www.MozarkPress.com
www.lsfisher.com

EARLY ONSET ALZHEIMER'S
MY RECOLLECTIONS, OUR MEMORIES

By L. S. Fisher

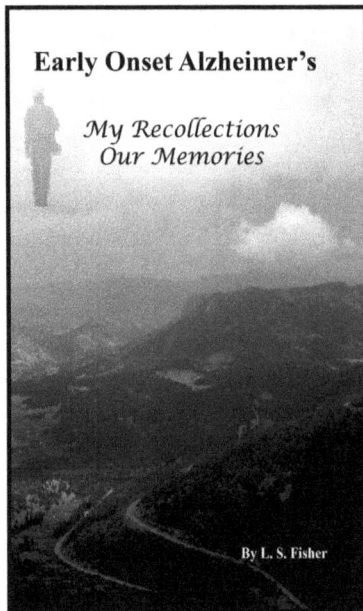

Mozark Press
PO Box 1746
Sedalia, MO 65302

www.MozarkPress.com
www.lsfisher.com

FOCUS ON THE POSITIVE
INSPIRE, ENCOURAGE, AND INFORM

By L. S. Fisher

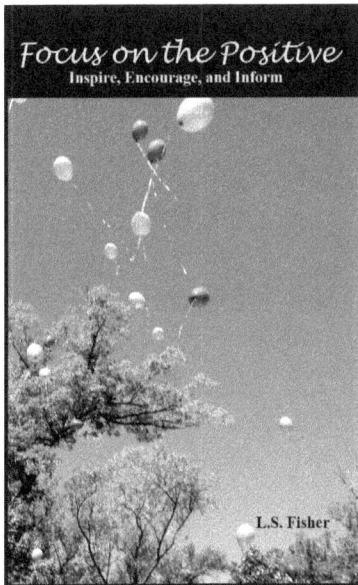

Mozark Press
PO Box 1746
Sedalia, MO 65302

www.MozarkPress.com
www.lsfisher.com

GARDEN OF HOPE
GROWING ALZHEIMER'S AWARENESS

By L. S. Fisher

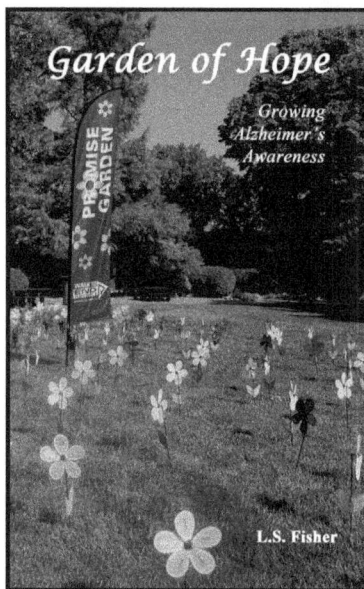

Mozark Press
PO Box 1746
Sedalia, MO 65302

www.MozarkPress.com
www.lsfisher.com

THE BROKEN ROAD
NAVIGATING THE ALZHEIMER'S LABYRINTH

By L. S. Fisher

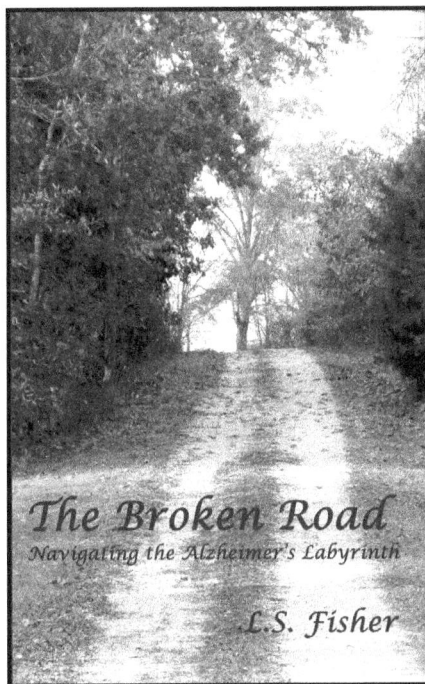

Mozark Press
PO Box 1746
Sedalia, MO 65302

www.MozarkPress.com
www.lsfisher.com

THE HEART REMEMBERS
EARLY ONSET ALZHEIMER'S ESSAYS

By L. S. Fisher

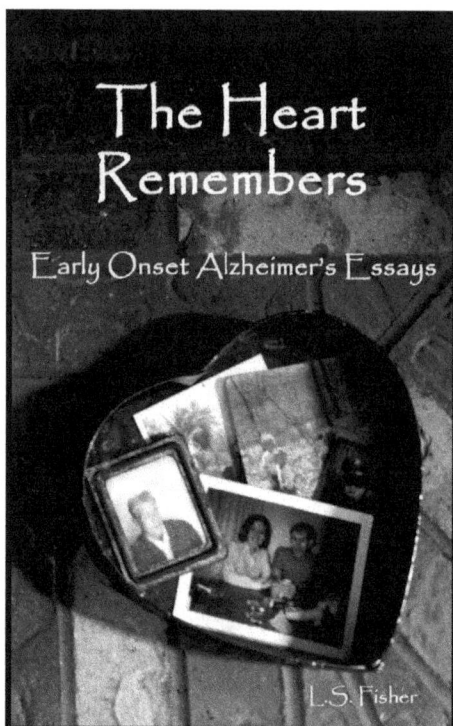

Mozark Press
PO Box 1746
Sedalia, MO 65302

www.MozarkPress.com
www.lsfisher.com

TREASURE TROVE OF MEMORIES
ESSAYS FROM AN AWARD-WINNING ALZHEIMER'S BLOG

By L. S. Fisher

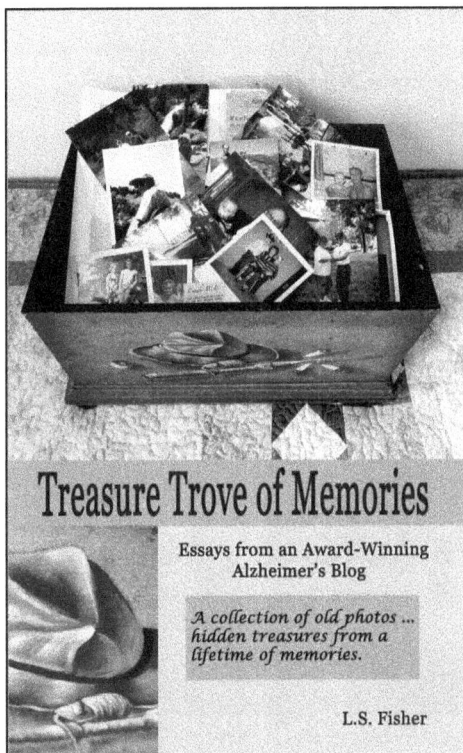

Treasure Trove of Memories

Essays from an Award-Winning
Alzheimer's Blog

A collection of old photos ... hidden treasures from a lifetime of memories.

L.S. Fisher

Mozark Press
PO Box 1746
Sedalia, MO 65302

www.MozarkPress.com
www.lsfisher.com

RUMINATIONS OF A CAREGIVER
ESSAYS FROM AN AWARD-WINNING
ALZHEIMER'S BLOG

Ruminations
of a Caregiver

Essays from an Award-Winning
Alzheimer's Blog

L.S. Fisher

Mozark Press
PO Box 1746
Sedalia, MO 65302

www.MozarkPress.com
www.lsfisher.com

Linda Fisher
Alzheimer's Speaker

Author and Editor
of
Alzheimer's Anthology of Unconditional Love

Linda is a longtime Alzheimer's Association volunteer and advocate. She speaks from her personal experience as a primary caregiver for her husband who lived with early onset dementia for ten years. She will speak to your group or organization about Alzheimer's or writing life stories. Choose from the following presentations, or request a different Alzheimer's or writing topic:

Writing as Therapy: Rocks and Pebbles

Where are your real life stories? Learn how to reconnect with the pebbles of your life and how writing these stories can be therapeutic. Discover slice-of-life moments that only you know. Suitable for senior adult writing groups, caregivers, and support groups.

Alzheimer's Voices of Experience

Learn about Alzheimer's from short excerpts of the heartfelt stories collected in *Alzheimer's Anthology of Unconditional Love*. These true stories allow you to glimpse the lives of real people who have embarked upon an unwilling journey into the world of dementia. This presentation gives a face and voice to the statistics of a baffling disease. Suitable for nursing home staff, caregivers, Alzheimer's staff and volunteers, civic organizations, and people who want to know more about dementia.

Alzheimer's Can Happen at Any Age

A PowerPoint presentation that focuses on raising awareness that Alzheimer's is a neurological brain disease and not a normal part of aging. Suitable for nursing home staff, caregivers, Alzheimer's staff and volunteers, civic organizations, and people who want to know more about dementia.

Alzheimer's Caregivers: Survive and Thrive

A workshop to develop caregiver coping skills. Linda speaks from her personal experience as a primary caregiver for her husband who lived with early onset dementia for ten years. Suitable for caregivers.

Alzheimer's Caregiver Stress

A PowerPoint presentation covering signs of stress and stress management techniques. Linda learned coping skills from her personal experience as a primary caregiver for her husband. Suitable for caregivers and support groups.

Alzheimer's Communication: Hear their Voices

A presentation to develop communication skills. Linda draws on her experience as the primary caregiver for her husband and his difficulty communicating due to aphasia. Suitable for nursing home staff, caregivers, volunteers, and civic organizations.

Caregiver Emotions

This one-hour seminar will help you identify seven caregiver emotions and develop strategies to cope with the emotional rollercoaster. This presentation focuses on the Alzheimer's caregiver, but care partners of other serious ailments can benefit from this program.

To schedule a presentation:

Email: lfisher@lsfisher.com

From the Author

My therapist is on call twenty-four hours a day. Some of my most successful sessions occur in the middle of the night when I'm comfortable in my pajamas. I grab a pen and paper or fire up my laptop and write through my worries, hurt, or anger.

I began journaling when I was twelve years old, and knew that writing helped me collect my thoughts and look at my problems more objectively. After I married and began to raise a family, I put away my journals except for an occasional travel log.

When my husband Jim developed dementia at forty-nine, I felt the need to write again. Through the ten years of Jim's dementia, I kept a detailed journal, mostly on tape. When I later transcribed the tapes, I re-discovered a wealth of information to help me heal.

Just like talking to a therapist, writing eased me through the emotionally draining decade of Jim's illness. The power of the pen healed my spirit.

Gathering and editing stories for *Alzheimer's Anthology of Unconditional Love* gave me purpose after Jim's death. I'm still working on a memoir and hope these stories can help others along their journeys.

My love of writing complements my volunteer work and helps me focus on the power of positive thinking and action.

L. S. Fisher lives, works, and writes in Sedalia, MO. The greatest tragedy in her life led to her greatest accomplishments. If her husband had not developed dementia, she would have spent her days working and her evenings at home. Instead, she has been recognized locally, statewide, and nationally for her Alzheimer's Association volunteer work.

Website: www.lsfisher.com
Blog: http://earlyonset.blogspot.com

Essay originally published in *Bylines 2010 Writer's Desk Calendar*, Snowflake Press, www.bylinescalendar.com

MoZark Press

Sedalia, Missouri

Mozark Press is a small publishing company in central Missouri dedicated to producing quality paperback books. We will publish short story collections, inspirational works, anthologies, general fiction, and non-fiction.

Mozark Press plans to publish 1-5 new books per year that meet our standards. We expect manuscripts to be polished and error-free when submitted.

Contact us if you want to see your work in print, but haven't been successful with a major publishing company. Maybe you have considered self-publishing, but do not have the time or know-how to do it yourself. We've been there, done that, and wouldn't wish it on anyone.

We are interested in new or established authors. Mozark Press will partner with our authors. We will provide a complimentary author webpage for one year. We won't ask you to sign a long-term contract.

We do not accept unsolicited manuscripts. If you have a completed manuscript, you would like us to consider, send a query letter to:

Publisher@mozarkpress.com

M_OZ_{ARK} P_{RESS}

Sponsor of the Sedalia
Walk to End Alzheimer's
Since 2009